THE EXECUTIVE

UNDER THE EDITORSHIP OF
Alfred L. Seelye

THE EXECUTIVE
AUTOCRAT, BUREAUCRAT, DEMOCRAT

EUGENE EMERSON JENNINGS

PROFESSOR OF BUSINESS ADMINISTRATION

GRADUATE SCHOOL OF BUSINESS
    ADMINISTRATION

MICHIGAN STATE UNIVERSITY

HARPER & ROW, PUBLISHERS
NEW YORK and EVANSTON

To my father,
Henry H. Jennings

CONTENTS

Forms of Escape
The Neurocrat
Power, Order, and Love in the Neurocracy
The Flexible Executive
Executive Maturity Today

PREFACE

The problems of becoming an effective administrator needs to be weighed in the light of a special trend in our culture, namely, role anxiety or uneasiness. The relationship between individual and society today is characterized by a confusion of norms, a lack of clarity as to what society expects of individuals in the fulfillment of his role responsibilities.

The term *role* comprises the way others who represent social standards expect an individual to behave, the individuals' response to these expectations, and his expectations of approval if he acts in appropriate manner. These several expectations vary according to the positions a person occupies in society as boss, worker, politician, teacher, father, mother, child.

In the contemporary United States, precise definitions of particular roles have grown less clear while at the same time insistence that they be met is terribly acute. The confusion amounts to a kind of coercion that is registered upon the personality as anxiety or feelings of uneasiness and discomfort. With this widespread role anxiety, hostile competitive feelings are overstimulated, and the need for escaping from or defending oneself against the emotions involved is very great. Greater still is the need for making productive use of these emotions in order to avoid being overwhelmed by them.

During the last ten years the author has actively counseled businessmen about problems of role anxiety. During this period a gradual breakdown and diffusion of what constitutes the executive or administrative role has occurred. The executive has responded to this vagueness about what constitutes being a good administrator by the search for a right or best answer.

This kind of emphasis on "right" answers is a very special development, characteristic of our culture and apparently of very few other societies. Of course, this tendency has increased noticeably during the last fifty to seventy-five years. Few children have not been brought up on the precept, "There is a right and a wrong way to do everything, and you might just as well learn the right way now." So deeply ingrained among certain groups in our society is this custom that few children are capable of shaping their activities by desires rather than by "right thinking." "Right" usually represents a marriage between what is functionally efficient and what is morally good.

To be sure, some children seem to be less inclined to "right thinking" today than they were twenty years ago. But the older generation which occupies a high position in our society still feels a necessity to fit everything into an accepted code, and an inability to express desire without moral sanction. These top executives in turn encourage "right thinking" in their subordinates. The unstated assumption is that "right" action will be rewarded. Executive success is very much related to having a correct definition of what is an executive.

Now we may draw closely to the administrative predicament of our time. The uncertainty of what is expected of the executive draws upon this emphasis on "right thinking." In the attempt to make clear the executive role, many executives are searching for a comprehensive solution. We may suggest parenthetically but not irrelevantly that they are prey to scientists, scholars, merchandisers of ideas, and quacks who believe sincerely or otherwise that there is a "right" and a "wrong" way to assume the executive pose.

This book attempts to describe the uncertainty in the executive role and the several poses or styles that are being developed today, namely, autocratic, bureaucratic, democratic, that will presumably help clarify what constitutes good executive behavior.

In a previous book, *Anatomy of Leadership*, the individual was studied as a potential change agent or event-maker. The difficulties surrounding the job of making things happen were examined in the light of certain converging forces that prohibited the individual from making a maximum impact upon the character and direction of his group or organization. The administrator in business, government, and unions was viewed as being "all too executive," in direct contrast to the event-making qualities of his predecessor of years past.

The theme in *Anatomy of Leadership* in no way precluded studying the executive as an implementer, nor did it disparage the executive who could better implement programs than design grand schemes of change and progress.

In short, today both words *leader* and *executive* are nebulous and abstract. We have noted that societies label the activities of their people. The word *leader* is used by our society to label so many and varied activities that for all practical purposes it really describes nothing. Equally confusing are the words executive, administrator, and manager. What constitutes executive behavior and the several executive styles or patterns that exist today are critical questions that penetrate to the heart of national productivity, health, and welfare.

Acknowledgement must be accorded to Dr. Alfred L. Seelye, Dean of the Graduate School of Business Administration,

Michigan State University, who as advising editor of this series provided guidance and suggestions, and who as chief administrative superior afforded the necessary time to do the research and writing.

In this regard, Dr. David G. Moore and Dr. Dalton Mc-Farland were also helpful in liberating the author from departmental responsibilities in the course of manuscript preparation.

Special indebtedness must be accorded Dr. Ordway Tead whose wisdom and scholarship afforded a critical examination of this manuscript that led to making important improvements.

Perrin Stryker, friend and member of the Board of Editors of *Fortune*, has in the past years been a source of stimulation. His reading of the manuscript was helpful in its expedition.

The author feels grateful to Dr. Paul Smith, Director of Studies, Graduate School of Business Administration, Michigan State University, whose experience as a former businessman was brought to bear as advisor and reader.

My wife, Marilynne, graciously substituted for the author as father while he proceeded to give birth to this next addition to the literary family. Her preparation of the manuscript, reading, and correcting were without substitute.

The book is dedicated to my father whose character weighs heavily upon the printed pages of this manuscript.

EUGENE EMERSON JENNINGS

East Lansing, 1962

THE EXECUTIVE

CHAPTER 1

THE BLURRED EXECUTIVE IMAGE

An uncomfortable feeling of uncertainty besets the men who sit behind the administrative desks in the high offices of organizations in our society. The delightful unambiguity of the past has been shattered by the imprecise and transitory present and the unpredictable future. The men in the centers of communication networks receive information, weigh probabilities, and make decisions about problems and events which make the activities of their predecessors seem earth-creeping in comparison.

The executive life, particularly in the large business or governmental organization, is a vigorous test of emotional maturity. Few who enter this life know just how close they may come to being pulled away from their emotional anchorages. The stress and strain in the executive role is reflected in the almost universal search for an ideal of effective executive performance. Many feel that finding this ideal will provide a comprehensive solution not only for particular problems, but for all problems that involve executive responsibility. The growing number of executives who are sincerely concerned about or overly preoccupied with determining what properly constitutes the executive role requires that we examine the men who occupy the glass and marble offices of our many public and private organizations.

The executive today faces the crucial and growing problem of finding the path to follow to control and direct human activity. Traditionally the unit of control has been the individual. From this unit flowed commands to which other individuals responded. This autocratic view, which meant self-rule or one-man control, was highly esteemed when organizations were many in number and small in scale.

However, for many reasons our society grew and became populated with large, complex organizations which taxed the limitations imposed upon the individual. It became apparent that the solitary decision-maker had to delegate his authority to subordinates who could specialize in areas of administrative importance. To keep the decision-making process from reverting to numerous unrelated one-man acts of control, an attempt was made to develop a system of policies and directives which, ideally, distributed the competency of the autocrat much as though he occupied simultaneously the several positions of authority. Whereas in the autocratic style of control the superior limited the authority of his subordinates through his personal will and control, in the bureaucratic style the superior limited the authority of his subordinates through routine, a set of directives, and specified responsibilities. Rule by rules partially took the place of rule by personal authority.

To the autocratic and bureaucratic styles was added an attempt to solicit ideas and advice from individuals who as a group were considered responsible representatives of the major interests involved. This style, which we shall refer to as democratic, attempted to make the decision-making process a function of the group as well as of the system.

With the successful introduction of group rule, the transition from the individual to the group as the unit of control seemed complete. Recently the president of du Pont stated that the responsible group had replaced the responsible individual and the welfare of the firm was better assured. But the transition is generally not that distinct. A modern organization cannot be without order and system, nor can it omit the personal authority and power of the individual. The individual, system, and group are today legitimate and useful instruments of executive control. They are all necessarily represented to some degree in the administrative routine of each executive.

The Strain in the Executive Role

The executive role has become fraught with difficulty. When one style was added, the other was not subtracted. Rather the increasing adoption of any one executive style seemed to draw adherents to the other styles. Consequently, a clear-cut image of effective and desirable executive style no longer exists. The three styles may stand out distinctly in theory, but their separate practical characteristics and advantages are less evident. Although the executive's effectiveness is largely dependent upon the conditions of his company, government, or association, his behavior cannot be treated simply as a human medium for the administration of internal problems of the organization.

In our interdependent society the modern, massive organization has a necessary interrelationship to the total society from which it derives its general character. And this society, which weighs so heavily upon the character of each organization, does not offer a great deal of help in providing a standard of executive effectiveness. It is too multifaceted.

It is a democratic society populated with representative institutions that are symbols of human freedom and dignity. Few nations have achieved the broad base of participation that affects our major issues and national policy. It is also a bureaucratic society, wherein order and efficiency have reached a level of productivity and affluence unmatched by any country in history. For a democratic society these feats of combining and organizing are without parallel. The diversity and inconsistency become excitingly apparent with the recognition of our autocratic patterns of control—great amounts of power rest in the hands of a few individuals whose decisions have national consequences as broad as those reached collectively. Autocracy is a broad cultural pattern that has enjoyed great prestige and social utility.

Our society reaps certain advantages from the rare union of these potentially antagonistic facets, but because of this complex combination it cannot provide a clear set of judgments about how to administer the many private and public organizations. Besides being multifaceted, and perhaps because of it, our society is whimsical and volatile in its reaction to administrators. It is quick to demand strong decisive executives and just as quick to condemn them for dictatorial methods. It appears to agree on the impersonality of the bureaucrat, but readily indicts the other two for their inefficiency.

The public behaves with such apparent volatility because the human is the least manageable of the animals. He neurotically sways back and forth between more and less control, never quite sure what he wants. But the habit of resisting control from others is no greater than the habit of refusing opportunity to participate. When people demand more voice in their own affairs, they are too often inclined to assume half-way measures of responsibilty.

It is not by accident that people live and work in organized systems with wills and efforts blended together. The executive, as we know him today, emerged largely because of the need to encourage people to go beyond that point at which they would normally stop. Many times along the way the resistance to the degree of control which we have today grew to rebellious proportions. The crises passed with the help of the people themselves who, torn between more and less control, could be persuaded of the former's advantages. But they always accept more control from others reluctantly. Administrators are viewed with ambivalence, with both love and hate.

The last two decades have seen a growing disapproval of the use and display of overt authority. The progressive classroom and the permissive home have attacked all traditional uses of authority, including that of clergy, parent, teacher, and administrator. This is the era of the good human relations man, who motivates through appeals to people's capacity to reason and be reasonable. Logic and understanding have pushed authority and force into the background. It is regarded as a sign of immaturity to administer in the home, school, church, or office by issuing arbitrary orders with expectation of instantaneous obedience. The autocrat seems to have been hurtled down the waste chute to oblivion. But with his demise the problems of control have not decreased. A society that has grown to disrespect overt authority is not easily managed.

The volatility of the public and changed attitudes toward authority only partially account for the strain in the executive role. There is also the crucial importance attached to maintaining a stable, productive economy. Before the Great

Depression the public generally believed that economic depressions were the inevitable workings of the business cycle. Today the public no longer believes that they are natural and inevitable, but rather man-made and hence avoidable. The public perceives the business, government, and union administrators of today as playing crucial roles in maintaining prosperity and high employment and in keeping down inflation. The public may not know exactly what must be done, but they keep a watchful eye on what their various administrators are saying and doing and are quick to criticize and distrust them. Fearing nothing quite as much as economic deprivation, the public looks to executives for their relief from insecurity.

The crucial role that the executive plays is also closely related to the fact that we are becoming a managed society. Rarely can an individual find the opportunity to be creative and productive outside of organization. Outside of organization there is simply more organization. If the typical individual is going to find his opportunity to participate in his society and achieve a sense of freedom, he must do so in and through his many and varied systems of social activity. Consequently, the individual looks to his administrators not only for freedom from economic deprivation, but for freedom to become creative and useful. The organization is emerging as the chief vehicle of democracy and the executive sits precariously in the driver's seat.

The executive has still larger moment in the unfolding drama of human history. The cold war means competition with communism on an economic basis. World peace and freedom will be won largely by raising the standard of living in friendly and uncommitted nations through sharing knowledge and services. For this responsibility business and government must acquire and develop administrators who are capable of seeing the total world situation and making decisions that enhance the well-being and prosperity of people who in the past seemed only distantly related to our national purpose.

This new responsibility is not easily assumed. For example, there are few universally accepted guide lines whereby the business executive can resolve the conflict between seeking and maintaining world markets abroad and protecting his own market at home from exploitation by foreign competitors. How does the executive serve his new mission to develop strong economies abroad without endangering a strong economy at home? Our economy at home must be strong to face the growing menace of communism abroad. But to win, we need help from strong nations abroad.

Many questions and problems which did not exist or were not consciously realized in the past weigh heavily upon the shoulders of the executive. The strain in the executive role has come from both unprecedented responsibility and uncertainty about exactly what that responsibility involves.

Administrative Anxiety

At this crucial time, when much of the future of freedom, human dignity, and material need satisfaction depends upon the executive's skills, there are few who exhibit genuine confidence about their ability to deal competently with administrative problems involved in running our public and private organizations. This administrative anxiety, which has replaced the profound certainty of the monarch of the past, is manifested in concern for new techniques and in threshing over systems of the past.

What one executive proposes, another refutes. To some the individual is the unit of decision-making, to others the group.

To some a clearly defined organizational structure is imperative, but to many it is a feature of administrative senility. Harold W. Sweatt, board chairman of Minneapolis-Honeywell Regulator Company, said about organization charts, "I hate them, they never work." J. Paul Getty of the large, complex Getty Oil Company said, "When you want it done correctly, do it yourself. I do it myself." John A. McCone, owner of Jasua Hendry Corporation, a shipping concern, Eisenhower's last Atomic Energy Commission chairman, and Kennedy's CIA director, said, "I am opposed to one-man rule." Eisenhower spoke of dictatorships as "very efficient." One cannot fail to be impressed by the confusion about administrative competency. Everyone is quick to point out the dangers. There are lions along one path, tigers along another, and snakes along a third. The only path where there are none is the pathological (see Chapter 8).

There is a gathering storm of criticism that the old enterprising spirit is passing and is being replaced by the cautious spirit of the bureaucrat. Lyndall Urwick and Northcote Parkinson, British management experts, feel strongly that the "civil service mentality" is rapidly spreading among business executives. Business firms are becoming top heavy with paper-shuffling, empire-building, and evasion of decision-making responsibilities. Government, which has usually borne the chief brunt of the accusation that we are breeding a nation of bureaucrats, is now being joined by religious, educational, union, and economic enterprises. The charge of growing bureaucracy in society is largely based on the belief that the essential creativity and spontaneity that we commonly believe have given us our affluence are receding as national ideals.

The question this accusation poses is whether our society can remain dynamic if its executives become less and less interested in bold action and more concerned with perpetuating their jobs and avoiding risk. Administrative anxiety is manifested in the crisis-like reactions to this acknowledged sapping of vital energy, inhibition of creative imagination, and curtailment of obedience and loyalty.

It was shocking to many to learn that Nelson Rockefeller's program, authorized by President Eisenhower in 1955, to enable the United States to seize the initiative in the cold war ran into opposition from state department officials, and after eight months of frustration Rockefeller resigned and recommended that the project be abandoned. He had been unable to get even a room set aside where maps, visual aids, and copies of the latest cables could be made available so that the president and his aides might be kept abreast of up-to-the-minute information concerning cold war developments. About this catastrophe Charles Stevenson remarked, "The stupidity that results when individuals become cogs in a vast bureaucratic machine bent on self protection and maintaining the status quo is compounded by an even more fundamental weakness: the appalling lack of understanding of Communism's complex tactics by key people handling our foreign policy, propaganda, economic aid, and overseas relations."[1]

This example of power conflict bears the imprint of flight from reality. In this instance in the crucial struggle with communism, our administrators failed to face up to their realistic responsibilities. But many critics' recommendations for change may be a similar flight from reality. Stevenson remarks, "We must have a cold war commander, working in close consultation with the President and heading a small professional staff of men skilled in total political warfare. They must have whatever authority is needed over the current operating departments to see that their orders are carried out instantaneously."

[1] Charles Stevenson, "What We Must Do to Win the Cold War," *Reader's Digest*, February, 1961, pp. 37–44.

The problems of immobility, lethargy, and conservatism in the face of impending national crisis, such as we face today, are broader than a single cold war commander can handle. Another bureau will not suffice. The unexpressed aggression which accumulates in a routine system of impersonal objectives becomes displaced upon programs and people and precludes their effective performance.

There is much danger in the belief that cooperativeness will be achieved by additional units or bureaus. Mr. Stevenson demanded that the units have whatever "authority is needed over the current operating departments to see that their orders are carried out instantaneously." The authority called for can flounder in a sea of gentle evasions, subtle and indirect obstructions, timely leaves of absence, and overwhelming information and arguments that can occupy an aggressive superior for his whole term of office.

Stevenson's suggestions are flight from reality if they fail to recognize how deep-seated are the impulses of self-protection and maintenance of the status quo. The extent of the bureaucratic order has not been well determined. Better known, however, is the anxious concern about its presumed pervasiveness and possible lethal consequences to our society and world.

Unfortunately, to call a man a bureaucrat is often to show disrespect for him. But equally disrespectful is the label of the committee man. There are many who feel that our compulsive tendency to consult with others and rely upon participation will be our ruination. *The Wall Street Journal* remarked, "If America ever does succumb to the Soviet, historians may record this contributing cause: The U.S. tried to defend itself with massed committees."[2] For some, the best committee is a one-man committee, and committees are often derisively de-

---

[2] *The Wall Street Journal,* January 31, 1958.

fined as groups that keep minutes and waste hours. A recent Senate subcommittee studying governmental machinery asked the Pentagon how many committees it had. The defense agency sent back its reply in a book the size of New York City's phone directory. Among the more than 900 committees are the Joint Master Menu Board, the Fiscal Sponsors Committee of the Toxicological Information Center, the Interdepartmental Screw Thread Committee, the Department of the Army Accelerated Item Reduction Program Task Group, and the Helium Policy Committee.

There are committees on top of committees on top of committees. In business and industry special executives may do nothing but keep track of committees and what they are doing. An executive is a nobody unless he has a committee and he simply cannot play the role of a competent executive unless he is surrounded by committee members. Even Richard Nixon succumbed to the urge to identify his competency with committees. Early in the campaign of 1960 he set up a group of advisors to function as a focal point for the campaign—with members interchangeable according to needs. As anxious as he was to be thought competent, he was equally anxious not to become known as a committee enthusiast. He called his group a board of strategy and announced that he would hold tight the reigns. Thus he attempted to prove himself the master of the executive dilemma—he could, like almost everyone else of any worth, establish committees, but they certainly would not tell him what to do.

The Pentagon is an extreme example of what many people believe is a general cultural pattern. They say we are overcommitteed. The prescription for what is to be done about "the mess in the Pentagon" usually varies with the view the individual has about the role of an executive. Donald Douglas, board chairman of Douglas Aircraft, prescribes, "What we need is more guts and less gobbledegook." President Kimball of Aerojet advises, "I would get rid of about three-quarters of the people in the Defense Department. Maybe that is not enough. Maybe it should be 90 percent."

The National Hot Seat

Some suggest the surgeon's scalpel and others the butcher's cleaver, but all seem to agree that bold, aggressive action must be taken if our society is not to be "committeed" to death. In effect the individual should be the master.

But what an alternative! Few styles are as difficult to master as that of one-man control. Howard W. Smith was the complete master of a committee, and as a result he was called dictator and was the object of considerable efforts to have him removed. Judge Smith, an old-fashioned Southern Democrat, wields immense legislative power as the chairman of the House Committee on Rules, a body with so much power that it is sometimes referred to as a "third house" of Congress. His able, shrewd, ruthless mastery of the jungle of parliamentary rules made him immune to the autocratic advances of Speaker Sam Rayburn, who wished at times to throttle Smith's ability to keep liberal legislation from reaching the floor of the House. In 1961 the Rayburn forces, with a gentle shove from President Kennedy, squeaked through a measure to expand Smith's committee from nine to twelve members. The move was aimed at constraining Judge Smith. Although Judge Smith maintains that the rules committee actually serves democracy because it allows an orderly pursuit of legislation and expression of views on bills prior to their presentation on the floor, it is definitely clear that his administrative style is not of the democratic cast. Nor does he pretend it to be.

For that matter, neither is the style of Rudolf Bing, manager of the New York Metropolitan Opera, Sir Lawrence Olivier, famous stage director and actor, or Thomas P. Kennedy, former New York City police commissioner. We shall note later how not one of these individuals has subscribed to the democratic style and, like Judge Smith, they have been severely criticized and denounced as dictators. Strong pressures are exerted against the style of one-man control. To argue that what we need are more men of decisive, vigorous character is to show ignorance of what autocrats have failed to do or of the burdens imposed upon them to thwart success.

For an example, let us return to the Pentagon, which is often pictured as the nation's hot seat. This tour of duty represents a challenge not yet successfully met by any executive. No defense secretary, no matter how decisive, has been able to come up with the right administrative formula. Charles Wilson, former General Motors president and fifth defense secretary, had the difficult job of retrenching after the Korean War. But he had to meet the emergency of the postwar downswing of defense appropriations. His autocratic style was insensitive to the tricky dimensions of the bureaucrat-ridden Pentagon. "Engine Charlie" heightened interservice rivalry and civil service mentality to the point that he left office probably the most hated secretary.

The seventh secretary, Thomas S. Gates, a Philadelphia investment banker, was probably more successful than any of his predecessors. He found a way to be both decisive and bureaucratically proper. Defense secretaries prior to Mr. Gates had the right to meet with the Joint Chiefs of Staff and the authority to make decisions about matters on which the chiefs did not agree. But none of them ever met with the Joint Chiefs and few of them exercized their power of decision. Gates became effectively decisive by joining the meetings whenever matters on which they disagreed were under discussion. In this way he was able to learn all the conflicting arguments and make a decision based on facts rather than on ignorance.

However, Gates had troubles too. For example, on November 16, 1960, President Eisenhower issued an order to cut the number of military dependents abroad in order to help cut off the flow of dollars from this country. Gates immediately asserted without apparent consultation that, although personal sacrifices would be needed, no loss in troop morale would occur because "our people are accustomed to sacrifice," and "we have the kind of leadership" that would ensure that troops make the proper sacrifices. But, in December, because of the furor in the office of Army Chief of Staff over the unnecessary and unfair need to ask troops to make this uncommon sacrifice, a deputy secretary of defense issued a memorandum to modify the controversial order. It took only one month to raise adequate pressure to restrain the hands of both the president and secretary of defense.

The pattern of Gates' relatively successful administration is a personal accomplishment and will not carry over for Robert S. McNamara, former president of Ford. On paper it would appear that he has great authority, but secretaries have often made the mistake of believing in their paper authority without considering the realities of the situation. The heads of the three overlapping and conflicting services, Army, Navy, Air Force, can go to powerful Congressmen, businessmen, and other secretaries when decisions go against them. At times they have been obstructionists to the point of making disagreement among them their art of managing the secretary. These men can start pressure campaigns through defense contractors and through leaks to newsmen; they can shift the battleground away from objective national interests to service prerogative; and they can overwhelm the defense secretary with information and arguments that often force him to call upon the president for help.

A high-ranking officer asked to explain a problem in an area totally unfamiliar to McNamara remarked afterwards that the new secretary appeared to believe that the Pentagon worked along lines laid down in the formal charts and along usual paths of human relationships. "What he did not seem to realize was the extent to which interservice interests and backstage knifings can warp normal ways of doing business."[3] Three months later, Secretary McNamara evidenced a "take charge" attitude—he alternately tapped gently and pounded away at the heads of the three services. An aide, describing a meeting with McNamara, reported: "He says he has decided this way or that way, then he tells you precisely what he wants you to do—A, B, C. It's all very polite, very considerate, and spine-tinglingly efficient."[4]

Before he took office he adamantly refused to appoint at least two men recommended by President Kennedy, and after he took office he immediately began to reorganize with more ambitious plans than any of the seven previous secretaries of defense. Already there are signs of the usual resistance to the autocratic fist that "Engine Charlie" often failed to hide in a velvet glove. As one high-ranking aide put it, "We are used to dealing with this [McNamara] type. He will prove manageable. We'll get him interested in something like political or public relations and from then on he won't bother us."

[3] Richard Fryklund, "McNamara—Can He Win in Untried Defense Role," *The Detroit News*, January 15, 1961, p. 12b.
[4] Jack Raymond, "Defense Chief Presses Unity," *The New York Times*, March 26, 1961, p. E7.

The Kennedy Path

Nothing seems to be filled with as much ambiguity as the problem of the American presidency. Everyone is getting his licks in on the president's problem of how to clear a way through the complexity of the United States government. There are all kinds of proposals for creating an "assistant president," or a "supersecretary of state," or a "council of wise men," which would take some of the burdens off the president.

However, the enthusiasts of the autocratic cast point out that these remedies would simply pile new complexities on old ones and give the president a greater administrative tangle to cope with. For example, each of the members of the president's existing cabinet has an immediate responsibility and, working together, they are supposed to provide a council of wise men available to advise the president on general policy questions. They are not always wise men. Often they wrangle among themselves and show a tragic lack of the broad view so needed to advise the president. By what reasoning will a "supercabinet" be any freer of human bias and ambition?

The autocratic enthusiasts argue that if the president has a weak secretary or a cabinet full of them, the remedy is to find a strong one and not to add another man or group of men to this weak link in the chain. Consequently, such advice as that of Governor Rockefeller to the effect that what is needed is a "superstrong" president is well received in some quarters and antagonistically rejected in others. The only certainty is that something needs to be done to bring some kind of order out of the chaotic state of administrative practice as it exists today.

In the midst of the conflicting views of the executive role,

President Kennedy stated clearly long before he was nominated what his style would be. In subsequent reports and events he has revealed a vigorous, steady determination to bring the departments in line by a strong, weighty hand of control. Remembering that the modern presidential campaign covers every issue from cranberries to creation, he said that the central issue upon which all other issues turn was not the farm problem or defense or Russia. It was the candidate's views of the presidency itself—his view of how its power and authority should be used. "Of course, a candidate's views on specific policies are important, but Theodore Roosevelt and William Howard Taft shared policy views with entirely different results in the White House." Noting that it is, of course, important to elect men of good intentions, Kennedy saw that Wilson and Harding as well as Lincoln and Buchanan were men of good intentions. "But there is a Lincoln room in the White House and no Buchanan room."

Elements of the autocratic, bureaucratic, and democratic styles are scattered throughout the history of the American presidency. The Roosevelts, Wilson, and Jackson showed strong autocratic tendency; Hoover, Cleveland, and Polk, bureaucratic; and insofar as they were willing to allow congressional committees and representatives of various interest groups to shape decisions, the presidents during the twenty years preceding Jackson were somewhat of the democratic style.[5] Half a century later Garfield was so anxious to keep harmony and respect and recognize the various claimant groups that he multiplied his duties to the point of appearing to be

[5] It must be emphasized that the author does not believe these men can be categorized into any one type. These tendencies are highly relevant to the situation and the inherent capacity to be so motivated. See the cautions provided at the start of the chapters on autocracy, bureaucracy, and democracy.

simply a registering clerk of the Congress. "Lincoln was a democrat as well as a dictator."[6]

Dwight Eisenhower brought to the presidency a particular style that like so many cases is very hazardous to classify. He could turn to his subordinates—his chiefs of staff, cabinet officers, and undersecretaries—and direct them to argue out the issues and bring him a decision. This view of executive behavior enlarged the decision-making process to include many executives. He ruled through an administrative core which at times acted superior to him. His "laissez faire" allowed for a staff of executives who represented elements of the three executive styles. Both Humphrey and Dulles were autocrats who ran one-man shows. They dominated the president, never consulted with department staff members, and tended to browbeat opponents.

Dulles' successor, Herter, announced upon taking office that he was a team man and for the most part made the decision-making process more collective than it had been in several decades. It was so collective that a year later when questioned by a Senate committee on who made the tragic decision to send Eisenhower to Japan in the face of apparent hostility, Herter replied that it was a collective decision, but if someone must be blamed, he would accept the blame.

Each executive must recognize that his basic problem concerns the view he entertains about his role. Knowing this, however, does not solve the problem. The views from which to choose are not easily incorporated into an effective administrative format. Kennedy, however, spoke with great assurance as to the view which he seemed to favor. He will act on the image of Abraham Lincoln, who when summoning his

[6] See Clinton Rossiter, *The American Presidency*, Harvest Books, 1960, p. 101.

wartime cabinet to a meeting on the Emancipation Proclamation said, "I have gathered you together to hear what I have written down. I do not wish your advice about the matter— that I have determined for myself." To assure his audience that he, Kennedy, was of the autocratic cast, he pointed out that this cabinet to which Lincoln issued his self-determined proclamation was carefully chosen to please and reflect many elements in the country.

No doubt Kennedy is set on the view he will incorporate into the executive format of the White House. After eight years of Eisenhower's laissez faire, with heavy bureaucratic overtones, Kennedy will probably be welcomed by the many executives who, in trying to make sense of the confusing situation, look to administrative figures for cues. No doubt they will find in him strong elements of the autocratic approach. But neither he nor any executive can long operate effectively without judiciously incorporating elements of the other two.

The Hughes Path

One cannot talk away the need to be orderly and cooperative as well as decisive and firm. A swing too far in any direction creates administrative instabilities that add to the administrator's anxiety. There are times when the lack of a strong hand may have tragic consequences. An example is the manufacturer's nightmare of General Electric's Hotpoint division. In 1959 it awoke to find sales of laundry appliances slipping to a miserable low despite an industry-wide pick up. The 1955–1957 models were so defective that to save its reputation the company decided to repair and replace 40,000 ailing machines that had brought complaints from owners. The cost was somewhere between $7,000,000 and $10,000,000.

Hotpoint's administrative problem was a case of too many cooks who often failed to agree about the ingredients that should go into the broth of washers and washer-dryer combinations. Because a competent chef failed to press his hand authoritatively, the top executives tried a little bit of everything, depending upon the extent of disagreement. When an organization needs a decisive executive, the need may not be a limited one.

Whereas the missing ingredient in the Hotpoint recipe was an autocrat, the next case shows what can happen when an ineffective autocrat is incapable of embracing any other style. Howard Hughes' absolute control of Trans World Airlines was taken away from him in order to gain from banks and insurance companies a $265,000,000 refinancing program. Ernest R. Breech of Ford, Irving S. Olds of United States Steel, and Raymond M. Holliday, financial vice-president under Hughes, formed a trust to vote Hughes' stock. Such control was given the trust because the banks no longer had faith in Hughes' administrative style.

Hughes is an autocrat who cannot make up his mind—a combination that almost always spells tragedy. Crises emerged which forced him to take drastic measures, which in turn obviated his chain of command. Hughes is temperamentally unsuited to establishing a bureaucratic system that affords continuity and stability. His whimsical and erratic interventions in subordinate executive operations precluded the development of a responsible administrative team. "Suspicious and withdrawn, elusive to the point of being almost invisible, he is loath to give anything up, loath to admit error."[7]

7 "The Hughes Story," *Fortune*, January, 1959, p. 80.

Despite the need for group consultation, Hughes exerted much of his control by long-distance telephone with executives who sometimes had not talked with him face-to-face for months. When decisions had to be made, he often called his chief executives from a pay booth in a filling station days or weeks later about some altogether different and usually trivial matter in which he had momentarily lost perspective. It is not incidental that often he had to borrow the dime to make the call.

The consequences at stake are of national significance, because besides Trans World Airlines Hughes owns Hughes Tool Company, the principal supplier of one of the oil industry's most important tools, and Hughes Aircraft Company, the country's largest manufacturer of electronic equipment for the military. The Hughes Aircraft Company, which is truly a national resource, was brought to the edge of ruin by its illusive and irrational administrative format. Airforce Secretary Talbot was largely instrumental in helping Hughes through the crisis, although Hughes did not receive his help well.

To say that Hughes is unorthodox is not an adequate excuse or explanation. Orthodoxy in administration is no longer crucial or common. Executive styles are flourishing with increasing diversity and richness of innovation. In this "executive renaissance" there are no acknowledged arbiters of style and any style goes as long as it is successful. Hughes failed to develop a realistic style that provided an effective approach to his problems of administration.

He is not alone in this problem. He is worthy of mention only because of the degree of his inability to blend autocracy, bureaucracy, and democracy into an effective style. All executives face this challenge to some degree and many flounder before they finally achieve a satisfactory resolution.

International Patterns

The problem of acquiring an effective executive view is not limited to our society. One needs only to observe the administrative mannerisms of the national figures of the world to note how these three themes are explored and experimentally used. The following discussion is not intended to be an exhaustive account of changing administrative views and styles of national figures of free and communist countries. It merely indicates that there is no uniform pattern, and perhaps there has never been. Also, political ideology and administrative behavior must be distinguished. The personal administrative behavior of the public or private administrator may be totally unrelated or at considerable variance with the political ideology of the government. Consequently, there are no firm guide lines, neither in our society nor the world at large, as to what constitutes the proper view of the executive role.

Russia, the most totalitarian of states, wherein you would expect to find executive behavior uniformly ordered along autocratic lines, is showing a strong general tendency in the direction of bureaucracy and democracy. Stalin, who once was described by Lenin as too rude and arbitrary, ran a tight one-man show. He consulted no one, used fear to keep subordinates in line, and allowed no one the luxury of self-expression. Khrushchev, however, seems to be in a period of executive experimentation.

Khrushchev had strong interests in organization and immediately set about to decentralize authority and responsibility. He saw that the Soviet economy had become too large and complex to be administered without the bureaucratic skills of functional authority, coordinated specialization, systematic planning, and liaison communication. In condemning the cult of personality, Khrushchev began to heed the advice of experts on a scale unheard of under Stalin's regime.

Besides incorporating the bureaucratic mode into his executive style, he has showed signs of depending chiefly on manipulation, persuasion, and the maintenance of respect on the part of his subordinates for their chief. Rather than mere mechanical execution of orders from above, officials under Khrushchev have been called upon to show initiative within certain limits. He encourages them to achieve a sense of participation, to act as members of the ruling authority, and to be in on decisions concerning matters according to rules and directions. It was the impression of one expert traveling in Russia that the decision-making procedure now legitimizes real discussion and difference of opinion within a small authoritative body.[8] Though, of course, if Khrushchev feels that his power is in any way threatened, he will assert his control by overruling his committees—just as Truman and Eisenhower, members of a democratic society, have been known to do with their committees.

By his routinization of the decision-making process through the systematic elaboration of rules and regulations and by developing a limited but effective participation base, Khrushchev is moving in the direction that executives, irrespective of organizational circumstances, are moving in the free world. He comes closer to Lenin's demands for someone more polite and patient and attentive to comrades and, judging from his personal behavior as an executive, comes closer than any other Russian power figure to behaving like many executives who head corporations and governments in the democracies.

The British are experiencing a substantial change in the

[8] Robert C. Tucker, *Impression of Russia in 1958: A Trip Report*, Rand Corporation, 1958, p. 80.

character and practices of business administration which involves the adoption of ideas and techniques that are a move away from the autocratic approach. The adoption of technical aspects of modern management is perhaps the most obvious trend. But there is also a change in the position of the businessman, who is now achieving uncommon status and prestige. The Napoleons from the boards of industry and business are emerging in Parliament as dominant forces. Prime Minister Macmillan is a major shareholder in a publishing firm and former director of Monotype. Chancellor of the Exchequer Armory is director of Lloyds bank and manager-director of a firm of textile manufacturers. Butler, the chairman of the Conservative party, has been a director of the Courtauld textile firm. The new trend is for the minister to be a self-made businessman. Paymaster General Mills, Defense Minister Walkinson, Minister of Trade Errol, Minister of Works Nicholls, Postmaster General Bevins, and Minister of Transport Maples are examples of the new pattern of weaving together the economic and political top brass of the country, much the same as in the United States cabinet.

These executives have to show administrative flexibility. The British cabinet system is basically pluralistic, with the cabinet assuming responsibility as a whole. Yet these former business tycoons are accustomed to taking charge and delight in making their own decisions. How they blend self-rule and team cooperation into an effective executive style within the British bureaucratic structure will be crucial to the future of both business and government.

In China, too, there have been unprecedented changes in administration. In 1961 the peasant in Communist China suddenly found some of his long-standing grievances acknowledged and his advice welcomed by the leadership in Peiping.

This trend parallels the growing resistance of low-level bureaucrats in many communist countries, including Russia, Yugoslavia, and Poland. The development in China followed the disastrous setbacks to the communist agricultural program in 1960 and the resultant food shortage. It remains to be seen whether the autocratic hand of top administration is wielded only after "counsel is first sought humbly."

In contrast to these real or apparent changes in the personal administrative styles of world figures are those who vary little from their earlier patterns of behavior. In spite of Field Marshal Montgomery's belief that De Gaulle has "mellowed" in recent years, he still brooks no opposition. He will go to the people for a mandate to approve his one-man acts of control rather than build around him a team of strong but supportive executives to manage effectively the clumsy military and governmental bureaucracies of France.

A similar problem exists in India. Whereas Gandhi was a superb judge of human character and surrounded himself with brilliant, capable men, Nehru has tended to surround himself largely with yes-men who rationalize and cloak his impulses and feelings in appropriate words. The old autocrat, Gandhi, listened to advice and accepted contradiction and criticism with patience. Nehru is impatient of criticism and is inflexible in his administrative view, which has not changed since he came to power. These are strong signs that suggest that Nehru's administrative technique will be considerably less effective as time wears on unless he does change substantially.[9]

In West Germany the compulsion for security through obedience and order has created an extreme contrast to the general administrative scene. The German executive style has

[9] For one view of the situation in India, see Amaury de Riencourt, "The Future of India Without Nehru," *Esquire*, May, 1960, pp. 104–108.

traditionally been autocratic with paternalistic elements. Top management is despotically thorough, burdening itself with details. Middle management is still regarded as a group of hired hands rather than as a repository of promising talent. The group is hardly more than a mechanism through which top management passes its orders.

The Germany that bred Bismarck and Hitler is not ready for the change depicted by many national leaders and administrators of the west. There is a clearly developed executive style to which many give deference—observe rules, take no initiative for adjusting them when anomalies crop up, and quickly give to higher authority the task of straightening out the slightest scrapes.[10] Unwillingness to challenge authority, admiration of discipline for its own sake and general indifference toward personal responsibility hinder a genuine movement away from autocracy. Politically West Germany has all the democratic trappings, but it is run by autocrats who have as firm a hold on the reins as any dictator. Adenauer is often called the "Democratur" because he appears to rule autocratically while bearing the label of democrat.

In business there are a few signs of deviation from this inflexible adherence to the autocratic executive style. Heinze Nordhoff, Volkswagen's managing director, and Joseph Neckermann, head of what might be called the Sears, Roebuck of Germany, are prodding the ever so slight gradual change. Just recently the aristocratic rulers of the 147-year-old Krupp industrial empire appointed Berthold Beitz of lower-middle-class stock to the post of president. Although be believes that, "There has to be only one boss, and I am this boss," his style is uncommonly easy-going and anti-Ruhr to the point of jab-

[10] Flora Lewis, "West German Democracy: Polite Yawns," *Milwaukee Journal*, November 1, 1959, p. 143.

bing his aristocratic directors and preferring to talk with factory foremen, shop stewards, and apprentices. It remains to be seen how much Monarch Alfred Krupp and his aristocratic directors can bend this fledgling premier to their will.

The Need for Courage

In the midst of all this world-wide change and experimentation one thing seems certain. As executives in all countries move away from their traditional administrative styles, the problem of how to act administratively becomes more difficult. Experiences in Britain and particularly the United States, where administrative reforms are more advanced, show that the ambiguity of the executive role is minimal when one style is uniformly practiced. As Khrushchev attempted to instill genuine committee activity into the deadly bureaucracy he inherited from Stalin's regime, the administrator was torn from the unambiguous condition of doing only what he was told to do within the rules and regulations of the system. The new freedom and responsibility were unwelcomed by many, abused by others, and they have made Khrushchev's administrative problems extremely difficult.

It seems clear in our own society that as dissimilar and potentially conflicting styles come into practice, the strains involved in the administrative role greatly increase. In such times of uncertainty there is a strong desire to return to the delightfully unambiguous condition of the past or reach for a comprehensive solution that promises to resolve all the conflicts that arise from the strain in the executive role. Either step is regressive and represents a flight from reality. The strain of the executive role may not be avoided; it must be faced constructively.

In this book we shall be concerned with the crucial problems that intensify the ambiguity and uncertainty of the executive role. Although primarily oriented toward the businessman, much of what is discussed has widespread application to understanding the executive role in government, education, church, social organization, and community enterprise. Because political events are better publicized than business, many examples will be drawn from the experiences of political figures.

Regardless of the context, administration means dealing with the deep psychological needs of men as represented in autocracy, bureaucracy, and democracy. The executive role is symbolic of our world today, caught between the rising forces of autocracy on the one hand and democracy on the other, each wielding clumsily the dull instruments of massive bureaucracy. The world awaits the final resolution fearfully and anxiously. The executive in whose small world these same forces swirl with demanding intensity must find his own resolution. We shall see that this has become for many a supreme act of faith and courage.

CHAPTER 2

THE EXECUTIVE DUALITY

There is a natural dilemma in the human situation. Man knows his existence is temporary and at the same time he strives for permanence. Perhaps in an attempt to compensate for his finite position, the individual strives for certainty. But because it becomes so important to find certainty he may grasp at what is not true. The duality always remains—the individual seeks resolution, but resolution never achieves permanency.

The administrative dilemma can be interpreted in similar terms. The role of the executive is uncertain—respected one day, he may be attacked the next. Feeling temporary he strives to achieve permanency. The duality is never resolved, but the struggle continues. To succumb completely would be to fail at the central task of being an executive.

The executive life is filled with uncertainty because it touches impulses of love and hate. By directing and controlling human activity the executive helps to provide channels through which human energy is given productive release and form. He excels in the art of making work and getting others to work, in providing a product or service to his customer or society. But his task would be lighter if his only problem were to help release energy that normally seeks productive expression. Work and the use of the products of work are also means whereby the destructive impulses of men may be sublimated into productive and desirable forms.

The executive is symbolic of modern massive organization. His skill in finding more efficient human combinations has been of great importance in developing and sustaining the modern systems of business and government. Because of his central role, he is the object of much of the ambivalence that people consciously and unconsciously feel toward those who determine and restrict their opportunity to be aggressive and creative.

The Myth of Ken

The executive exists in a system of power and order. The instruments of power made available to him by his responsibilities must be both guarded and guarded against. This duality of opposing conditions cannot be avoided.

The duality of the executive role may be illustrated by the myth of ken. In ancient Egyptian the word *ken* meant strong-weak—a recognition of the fact that all men contain within themselves this essential duality or contradiction.[1] Eventually, the double meaning was divided into the two concepts of strong and weak. The two different meanings were conveyed by using different pictures following the symbol for *ken*. The picture of an upright, armed man next to the word *ken* meant strong, and a picture of a crouching, weary man meant weak. To be strong was to be in an upright position and armed with the tools of power and authority; to be weak was to be bent

[1] See Sigmund Freud, "The Antithetical Sense of Primal Words," *Collected Papers*, vol. 4, Basic Books, 1959, pp. 184–190.

over and exhausted from submission to the requirements of work. To be above is to be strong and to be under is to be weak. Few people want to be crouched over, weary from the toils of servitude, but most have no choice.

However, throughout history people have engaged in a continual struggle to become strong or to control the strong. One of the most effective means for achieving strength was to establish institutions that guarded them against their rulers. Whatever their primary purpose, such institutions as religion, government, ritual, magic, and medicine have included vital ingredients to guard the weak against the strong. They represent man's ancient attempts to achieve a satisfactory resolution of the duality of power.

Taboos on Rulers

Another illustration of the duality of power may be seen in the primitive taboos on rulers. The chief was believed to possess a mysterious and dangerous magic power. The power itself was ethically and morally neutral, that is, it could be used for constructive or destructive purposes but was not constructive or destructive in itself. Through the use of his power, the chief controlled the happiness and welfare of his subjects. As Freud says, "he is a person who regulates the course of the world; his people have to thank him not only for rain and sunshine, which allow the fruits of the earth to grow, but also for the wind, which brings its ships to the shores, and for the solid ground on which they set their feet."[2] Because of his importance to the very existence of his subjects, the chief, and his power, had to be carefully guarded from every conceivable danger. At the same time, his subjects had

[2] See A. A. Brill, ed., *The Basic Writings of Sigmund Freud*, Modern Library, 1938, p. 839.

to be guarded against the chief, for his power was so strong that it could bring death and destruction upon contact to anyone not protected by a similar charge. Thus a system of prohibitions and prescriptions developed around the person of the chief to guard and guard against his power.

Freud noted that the Nubas of East Africa believed that they would die if they entered the house of their priest-king, but they could escape this danger if on entering they bared the left shoulder and induced the king to touch it with his hand. This act indicated submission to the king, as opposed to a direct approach which might represent a threat to him. The subject was therefore protected from the potentially destructive power of the king by passive behavior. It is not unlike our custom today of knocking or gaining approval before entering a room to show subservience to the boss.

The king's touch could be constructive as well as destructive. We find examples of the belief in its power in our own civilization. Charles I of England presumably cured a hundred sufferers of a disease called "the king's evil." Under Charles II royal healings of scrofula attained their greatest vogue. The "laying on of hands" is still practiced by many religious leaders. Thus, the king or chief seems to be endowed with a godlike power and ability to bestow all wealth and happiness.

Freud noted the seeming contradictions involved in the taboos concerning rulers. Why should persons of such perfection of power require such elaborate protection against threatening dangers? One possible reason was that the king existed only for his subjects. His life was valuable as long as he discharged the duties of his position by ordering the course of nature for his people's benefit. Thus, the people went to great measures to protect him against threatening dangers. But there was a strain of fear and mistrust mingled with the motivation behind the taboo rules for the king. As soon as he failed to perform his duties, the religious devotion which was lavished upon him ceased and changed into hatred and contempt. "Worshipped as a god one day, he is killed as a criminal the next."[3] If their king was their god, he was also their preserver, and when he did not preserve for them, they made room for another who would. In this sense love and hate were rationally bestowed and withheld.

Ceremonious etiquette, prohibitions, and observances were not created for the other's comfort or for contributing to his dignity. They were a combination of protection and restraint. If anything, these rules and taboos decidedly detracted from his comfort, hampered his every act, annihilated his freedom, and filled his life with many sorrows. The king became hedged in by intricate human relationships and social regulations to restrain him from involving his people and the universe in one common catastrophe. In some societies resistance against accepting the so-called "kingly honor" became so great that many tribes were compelled to make strangers their kings.

In other words, this taboo on rulers practically canceled out their great privileges. Freud wrote, "They are privileged persons, they can do or enjoy what is withheld from the rest through taboo. But in contrast to this freedom they are restricted by other taboos which do not affect the ordinary individual."[4] But this contradiction reflects a basic consistency— a consistently ambivalent attitude toward power and authority.

Restraints upon the Executive

Ambivalence toward power figures is certainly still present in our society. The hostility may be repressed and not con-

---

[3] *Ibid.*, p. 843.
[4] *Ibid.*, p. 844.

sciously felt or directly manifested. It may be reversed and express itself in the form of exaggerated devotion or support for powerful people.

Every child experiences ambivalence toward his parents who are at once a source of love and punishment (see Chapter 4 for a more complete discussion). When the child is punished he naturally feels resentment bordering on hatred, but hating the one he loves creates feelings of guilt. His parents, school-teachers, minister, and community authorities hammer home the guilt by the principle of honor thy father and mother.

A mechanism becomes established whereby feelings of hate are repressed, reversed, or displaced. For this reason many adults may seem unaware that their behavior toward authority figures reflects unconscious reactions of love and hate. Their hostile reactions are often expressed in taboos and ritualistic devices that constrain the authority's use of power against them.

These taboos have reached tremendous proportions. New taboos are introduced and older ones are still maintained. The executive today is engulfed. It is as though he is being punished for his elevation. So deep and pervasive is the fear that he will make decisions that commit us against our will or better interests, that the moment the executive is placed in a position of power, a steady patter of restraining forces and regulations wears him down to less than primal proportions.

A case in point is the American presidency, which starts with the principle that one man is responsible and that his opinions are to dominate the administration. The founders were insistent on one-man control to the point of giving him qualified appointment power and absolute power of removal. But there were "guarding against rules," tendencies born of an ambivalence toward power figures. The congressional legislative system acts as a check on the power of the chief executive. He executes the laws passed by the Congress and performs the duties prescribed by the Constitution, but he is not above the law and cannot create new laws arbitrarily. This system specifically guards against the use of power leading to tyranny such as that which preceded the American Revolution.

The same pattern is followed for all other executives in business or government. They must use their power, but their power must be controlled. They must never be allowed to resolve the duality of their position permanently—it is always to be a combination of strength and weakness. The problem illustrated by the myth of ken is always with them to hobble every potential act of aggression with a set of formal or informal restrictions.

The first president, Washington, did not abuse these powers which were in many ways tailored to suit his personality. As much as his sense of propriety allowed, he tried to defer and to consult, and seldom did he show lack of understanding for those about him. Although he formally asked for advice, he worked out his decisions in private. He was strong, firm, but considerate and fair.

But he did enlarge the power of the president by the rules of necessity which Jefferson later helped to develop. "Those who accept great changes have a duty to assume risks themselves on great occasions, when the safety of the nation, or some of its very high interests, are at stake." Men of strong autocratic tendencies further enlarged the powers of the executive office to the point where it is now the dominant authority in the land. Jackson, Lincoln, the Roosevelts, and Wilson were at some time called dictators and were ambivalently viewed and treated.

During many national crises the desire to guard against power may be momentarily overcome in submitting to the rule of a strong executive type. Franklin Roosevelt did much to develop a primal "law giver" function of the chief executive office during the many national crises of his regime. For this he was both hated and loved.

But because he alerted all to what one man could do with skill at resolving the duality of strongweak into a position of great power and strength, there have been strong pressures, rules, taboos, and regulations placed on the office of the presidency. With each election a bigger man is required to wield the instrument of executive powers effectively. The more successful he is, the more restraints placed on him. For example, he is now restricted to only two terms of office. The rationalizations for these restrictions range all the way from fear of dictatorship to the fear that one man may involve the rest of the universe in common catastrophe. The fear of a universal catastrophe is not essentially different from the primitive fear that the ruler's magical power was so great that it must be guarded against—only the form is different.

Hostility toward power and authority is sometimes so strong that capable men refuse to accept office and those who actively seek it are held in disrespect if not contempt. The political game called "the draft" is a contrived mechanism for getting a nomination or position without risking the disrespect that is often accorded the office-seeker. Before people give their support, they put the candidate through a kind of primitive ordeal that humiliates him, challenges his integrity, destroys his privacy, forces him to rid himself of financial and legal holdings and ties, holds him personally responsible for all acts committed after he achieved majority, and requires him to confess publicly any acts of moral transgression and impropriety.

However, even while we are putting our leaders through these ordeals, we may still confer our respect on the strong among us. We speak glowingly of their contributions and talents, their devotion to company, community, nation, and mankind. We honor governmental leaders with degrees, citations, special privileges. We accord them the formal dignity of rulers. But they are for all practical purposes subjects. So tightly are they woven into the total social fabric that they are never free of pressure to conform and to seek a common level of adjustment. They are well guarded against.

What are some of the common restraints in the institutional framework? If an executive mixes with his subordinates, he may risk loss of prestige and influence. He is provided a greater opportunity for privacy by such means as an office physically separated from the group and enclosed by soundproof walls and thick heavy doors. This separation inevitably contributes to mistakes and malfeasance. He is bothered and overburdened with all sorts of problems and kept so busy that he has little time to think and to enjoy himself and his family. To guard against him people build obsessive patterns of busy work and massive systems of detailed responsibilities. They destroy his mobility by courting his favor, seeking his approval, and becoming intimate and confidential to the point of binding his emotions.

The ceremony of group consultation also serves to guard against power. The rationale is, of course, administrative efficiency, but in many cases the effect is also to guard the interests of the group against the executive's "magic." Group meetings and conferences may take up more time than any other administrative function. Whereas at one time the executive had to be a prototype of decisiveness and wisdom, he must now avoid conflict, be popular, and engage in proper human relations. A fraternal organization is emerging to displace the patriarchal system of the strong men of the past.

The Fall of the Businessman

No society can withstand the effects of allowing some to have unguarded power. All must be "strongweak"—the duality must not be successfully resolved. The ambivalence toward authority and power is the heart of the duality found in the executive role. To control means to manage the human emotions of love and hate. In practice it may mean to build and maintain systems of effort rationally organized around inte grated goal achievement. It may mean hiring, training, supervising, communicating, remunerating, and releasing. It may mean running a business, government, school, or association. But whatever the executive's formal responsibility, the connections with the destructive impulses are close and clear. So preponderant are the human difficulties encountered in business, industry, education, and government, that the executive must always be concerned with the problems of morale, motivation, insubordination, indifference, and insecurity.

There was a time when the executive was not aware of how close he was to the strong aggressive impulses of men. The sensitive executive of today who is alert to human relations problems is quite different from his autocratic predecessor. One can hardly believe that the business executive sits in the same chair occupied by the "Robber Barons," the "Titans," the "Lords of Creation," as his predecessors were variously called. One must take a quick second look to realize fully that the instruments at his command were not too long ago wielded arbitrarily by a generalized sense of swaggering power. This was the age of the dinosaurs.

Commodore Vanderbilt's famous remark, "Public be

damned," recalls a past that the executive is desperately striving to disown. The businessman then believed that a self-regulating mechanism, an invisible hand, was operating to make growth, progress, and happiness an inevitable result. By pursuing the responsibility of making a profit, he was performing his greater service to his society.

In this period the best workers were hungry workers, their immediate superiors were considered unreliable and untrustworthy, and all power was centralized at the top. In moments of remorse these captains of industry looked to abstract theory for support of their belief that profits at all costs were their measure of virtue and righteousness. James J. Hill said that the fortunes of railroad companies were determined by the law of the survival of the fittest. John D. Rockefeller declared in a Sunday school address that his activities represented merely the working-out of a law of nature and a law of God.

When Andrew Carnegie became troubled and perplexed by the failure of Christian theology to support his business aggressiveness, he suddenly realized that he was participating in a great evolutionary struggle for survival. "Not only had I got rid of theology and the supernatural, but I had found the truth of evolution. All is well since all grows better, became my motto, my true source of comfort." Whereupon he turned to his society the same uncompromising face but with a greater sense of justification. This titan of the past was worshiped and respected as a hero by some, hated by others. In either case, he represented many of the values considered important. He was hard-working, ambitious, frugal, honest, and religious. People carried his business-like qualities into all their pursuits. Their respect and affection turned their thoughts away from the titan's tyrannical acts with workers and competitors.

The human indignity has been well recorded. Rockefeller

hired spies and saboteurs to destroy local competitors and to keep the employees in line. Ford kept employees nonunionized by systematic intimidation. His well-paid corps of spies and thugs detected and beat up workers who joined unions. It seems unnecessary to recall the image the titan presented to his society. It was in essence stern and decisive, with confidence in the inherent wisdom of the businessman's aggressive pursuit of profits.

The Great Depression set in, but the businessman, still certain that he had found the secret to prosperity, insisted on the right to pursue "business as usual." But the people began to disbelieve, and initial successes of a democratic reform movement backstopped by pump-priming social and economic legislation began to assert the authority that was previously ascribed to the "invisible hand." Slowly the public awoke to see irresponsibility and incompetency in the titan. Their repressed hostility, always to some extent ready to be unleashed on masters who control and direct their lives, came to the fore to be preyed upon by political and social reformers and opportunists. The rebellion was recorded by the rise to power of the twin giants of big union and big government.

The business executive was in a three-way squeeze between the interests of his firm, the demands of labor, and the watchful eye of government. The "countervailing power" that supposedly replaced the "invisible hand" did not make executive life easier. For example, the activities of powerful multiple-company unions with interindustry affiliation thwarted the ability of the single firm to compete. They encouraged the engaging of collusive activities among competition. United States Steel's chairman Roger M. Blough remarked, "Loyalties are divided and the integration of the corporation is imperiled where union represents employees of competing organization."[5] Many feel that the opportunity to conduct business enterprise is threatened by government which fails to understand what Blough calls the "dynamics of productive groups."

The Rise of the Enlightened Executive

Today's executive was in his formative years when businessmen were being violently attacked as enemies of society—greedy, grasping, dictatorial, antisocial. Cameron Hawley, a member for twenty-four years of Armstrong Cork Company and widely known for his best-selling business novels, *Executive Suite, Cash McCall, The Lincoln Lords*, suggests that, although not all these accusations were true, the young businessman saw enough truth in some of them to make him decide that when he got to the top he was going to be different. "Before long, we found a word to characterize that difference: 'enlightened.' "[6]

Consequently, the face the executive presents to the public now expresses social responsibility. However, without a framework for precise definition of his moral and social responsibilities, the executive is thrown into uncertainty. He must constantly feel the pulse of public opinion and be wary of alienation. Wherever he goes today he is accompanied by a host of survey makers, social engineers, public opinion analysts, and human relations experts. In short, he is becoming more sensitive to his environment. But as he becomes more sensitive a curious phenomenon begins to develop. He is reminded more and more of his precarious situation, of the problems created by his business and by business in general. He becomes more

[5] "The Steel Crisis," *Business Week*, April 25, 1959.
[6] See Cameron Hawley, "Needed: More Tough-Minded Leaders in Business," *Reader's Digest*, February, 1961, pp. 55–59.

self-conscious, more deliberative, more aware of the basic incompatibilities of his role and business.

His growth toward social awareness is an irreversible step. He must recognize the problems created by his society and the institution for which he stands. The more aware he becomes the less opportunity there is to escape the problems and return to the state of his autocratic predecessors.

The modern corporation, owned by thousands of stockholders, employing thousands of people, and serving millions of customers, is no longer a private institution. The old distinction between private and public interests has become dim and may disappear. An era of high administrative democracy may be about to begin.

This changing character means that as business serves more nonpecuniary goals, the qualifications of executive fitness become nonpecuniary too. Increasingly the executive must show his social and moral credentials for access to the power with which he is entrusted. Even then his power is kept in check by the many pressures arising from the new character of business enterprise. Nevertheless, he still has tremendous discretion and latitude. He is aware that he is subordinate to the many interests that choose to declare themselves from time to time. But, he is also aware that he must not become a vehicle for any one of these interests. He must achieve sufficient power and control over the many people he must also serve. The duality is intense and ambiguous.

He must be a parent, churchman, fund-raiser, patron of the arts, community elder, educational leader, political supporter, governmental servant, and public statesman. He goes to conferences, professional meetings, and university seminars; reads, speaks, and writes; counsels, trains, and prophesies.

The fastest growing element in public service today is the personal participation of businessmen. New York Telephone Company's president, Keith McHugh, devotes part of every working day and three or four evenings a week to civic activities. He often seems to be only a visitor in his own corporate domain. President Joseph B. Hall of Kroger Company cut the executive dining room out of plans for a nine million dollar headquarters building. He wants his executives to get out into the community at noontime. George Romney, former president of American Motors, works fifteen hours a day and fears that his stockholders may think the company's profit position would be brighter if he was not so active in community work, including his leadership of the Latter Day Saints that consumes nearly all of Mr. Romney's Sundays and part of his Saturdays.[7] In 1957 a *Management Methods* magazine survey showed that 76 percent of the executives it polled worked for bosses who encouraged them to be active in public service. A large number of companies now have executives with such titles as director of public and civic affairs.

In addition, the business executives may attempt to become politically oriented. United States Chamber of Commerce, American Management Association, many institutions of higher education, and hundreds of companies have set up courses for executives on grass roots political action and the ways and whys of political immersion.

In adopting humanistic goals and policies the executive is rebelling against the autocratic role of the traditional businessman, breaking out of traditional practices of authority, and defying established views of human nature. Those who still cling to the autocratic style, and there are still many who do,

[7] *The Wall Street Journal*, December 10, 1958.

see him as an immature upstart, a hypocrite, or a weakling who is incapable of assuming a properly firm, decisive approach to the conduct of business enterprise. But the executive's participation in the many activities outside of business may well be the way to master those aggressive forces unleashed against his predecessor during the "fall of the titans" in the Great Depression.

The broadened life is difficult. Moving in and out of his business and society presents complex problems, whose solutions are never clearly agreed upon by the various claimant interests. Problems of how, when, and whom to control and serve are greater. There are no arbiters of what is a proper stance before any of these groups. The executive lives today in ambiguity undreamed of by his predecessors.

The business executive is no longer a private figure. He is becoming totally immersed in his society. He operates from his formal position within his organization, and at the same time he has extended the sphere of his interest and responsibility to encompass issues and problems only remotely related to business enterprise. Unlike the titan who was preoccupied with his right to control, the enlightened executive is becoming preoccupied with his responsibility to serve.

The transition from control to service is not without hazard. To operate effectively he must not become overwhelmed by the complexity of his responsibility or by his growing prestige and respect. He is used in government, community, charity, and education. But he would be a fool to believe that these opportunities are what they may seem to be at first glance. People can control a man they fear by engaging him in many activities where he can be influenced as much by them as they are by him. The struggle in the myth of ken goes on in a more sophisticated atmosphere of subtlety and indirectness.

The Organized Life

The job of the executive is to find new and different ways for man to sublimate his aggressive drives into socially healthy and personally satisfying forms. If he does not do this task effectively, unexpressed aggressive drives will be directed against him once again to further restrain and confine his authority and power.

The biggest problem facing executives today is the lethal compulsiveness of modern life. If another explosive outburst occurs to shackle still further the freedom of the businessman to lead his institution, it will occur not because of some overt abuse of human dignity, but because a faceless, subtle tyranny has made all men into active idiots. When they awaken from their mesmerization, all hell will cut loose.

Everything is organized: play, work, family, community, charity, religion, education. From the moment of birth the individual is provided a well-ordered framework for experience and action. This tight order acting upon his natural dispositions makes him the person he is today.

The modern child has his hand held longer before he is released as an adult. And his release is merely a transfer into a different system of discipline and efficiency more regimented than what he has previously experienced. Everything is organized, managed, and rationalized from birth control to career development to retirement planning. In such a society the individual moves from one organization to another throughout his waking day. Two out of three live in urban communities, four out of six work in some twenty thousand businesses with an indicated worth of a million dollars or more. One out of ten of the actively employed work in government. Almost twenty million workers belong to unions of some kind. In fact, so total is the organization of our society that a union has been organized for the organizers of the International Ladies Garment Workers Union.

There are few activities that do not have an association. There are associations for the manufacture of cement bomb shelters and of automobile seat covers. In the last ten years more associations were developed to represent professional and nonprofessional activity than in all of the preceding hundred and fifty years. No one is alone—he is represented, regulated, and advised. There is an administration of some kind looking out for him. Big brother is no longer just around the corner, but rather holding his hand to make sure he makes the right turns.

Some of the studies of the American scene show that organization has become an end itself, and in some of the most unlikely activities. For example, one survey recently made for the Congregational Christian Church indicates that one third of the denomination's members approached religion as an organizational activity rather than an intellectual, spiritual, or devotional experience. They were active in the system, attended regularly, participated in church activities, supported church programs through voluntary service and contributions, but they did not approach religion as an opportunity to relate meaningfully to their God.

The organization has come to stand between them and God if not their fellow man as well. Even the Roman Catholic bishops of America, who represent a monolithic organization, sent out strong warnings in 1961 against the spread of uniformity of thought and supreme loyalty to the organization. They reported: "Pressures are growing for a constantly greater reliance on the collectivity rather than the individual. . . . An inordinate demand for benefits, more easily secured by the pressures of organization, has led an ever growing number of people to relinquish their rights and to abdicate their responsibilities." In churches, colleges, schools, and town halls, cries of warning are heard that men must not lose sight of their responsibilities toward each other as individuals.

Much of life revolves around the supremacy of the system and the subordination of self-expression and responsibility. The typical individual who does not meaningfully relate to others is nevertheless active all day. For example, he awakens in the morning to begin a routine movement through a labyrinth of rooms, each of which has acquired functional specialization. He has his bathroom, his children theirs; he eats food in another room prepared in still another by the technical marriage of a can opener pressing down upon a mounted can of ready-to-eat foods. In one room he reads, in another he watches television. If he could only find the right room, he might know how to behave.

He opens the door to grab the morning milk left at the door by an agent of a vast dairy and distributing system, whose corporate maneuver, so vital to his health, never consciously concerns him but is closely scrutinized by members of a governmental bureaucracy graciously looking after his interests.

Before leaving for work, he hurriedly scratches off his monthly payment on the mortgage, financed by a bank whose corporate activities are beyond his understanding, but which are also scrutinized by the gracious efforts of governmental inspectors. After kissing his newly born infant son, who is himself a product of planning and control, he dashes either into a transportation system whose civic mysteries he does not understand or into an automobile whose mechanical mysteries are equally beyond him.

At the factory or office he becomes a cog in a set of systems far beyond his capacity to control and understand. To him, as to everybody else, the company he works for is an abstraction. If he is a laborer he plays an unwitting part in the "creation of surpluses," and, though he does not know it, his furious activity at his machine is regulated by the "law of supply and demand," the "availability of raw materials," and "the prevailing interest rates." He does not know it, but he is headed next week for the "surplus labor market." A union official collects his dues, just why he does not know. At noontime that corporate monstrosity, the cafeteria, swallows him up, much as he swallows one of its automatic pies. After more activity in the afternoon, he seeks out a standardized daydream, produced in Hollywood, to rest his tense but not efficient mind.[8]

This individual has been active all day. He has been moved in a framework that leaves little room for free choice, spontaneous activity, and personal responsibility. Consequently, his complaints are numerous—bureaucracy at the office is stagnant, government is impersonal, our system of distribution has become immoral hucksering, advertisizing is sex without reason, television is beneath contempt, our prosperity breeds insecurity.

Everything seems wrong, but even this feeling cannot be adequately expressed owing to the adjustment motif that says he should relax and enjoy it all, he never had it so good. A tranquilizer pill swallowed with a gulp of "Metrecal" puts him to bed next to a television that turns itself off automatically. He awakens the next day to climb into the same framework of well-ordered activity.

Our society and work is becoming for many people monotonous and impersonal. It would seem that the executive's social responsibility must take account of the fact that mere

---

[8] I am indebted to Gordon W. Allport for parts of this revealing description of modern man. See *Personality and Social Encounter*, Beacon Press, 1960.

cogs in vast impersonal systems are sources of inefficiency, hostility, and irresponsibility at work. The executive must realize that the ability of people to live and work productively depends increasingly upon their being more than merely busy and orderly. They must participate actively in determining the conditions whereby they are busy and orderly.

The executive must broaden the base of his administrative format because the continued productivity and morale of those with whom he works is at stake. To repeat, when everything is organized, people increasingly depend upon those who control and direct them for much of their opportunity for self-expression. No longer are there interstices of freedom outside the large organization, for the simple reason that outside the organization there is simply more organization. The organization must be viewed as the major vehicle of democracy and the executive as democracy's chief actualizer. Democracy must largely shape the executive's view of his administrative responsibility.

The Pessimistic View

There is widespread pessimism that the executive will not be able to direct and control the aggressive impulses which are finding increasing expression in union demands, governmental regulations, antibusiness hostility, and the many taboos against the instrumental use of his power and authority. The future is not clearly in favor of the business executive's continuing to operate his firm as he has. Already he is so boxed in from all sides that he is incapable of making self-determined choices. Things may get worse and may not ever get better.

There is in many quarters a growing antagonism toward big organizations in general, unions and government as well as business, and if these hostile tendencies have anything in com-

mon at all, it is the belief that man is straining under the yoke
of powerful, impersonal systems of control that do not allow
sufficient expression of human needs and ambitions. All
executives, whether public or private, share this acute problem
of administration. The peculiar condition of a managed society
is that administrative efforts in one area impinge upon efforts
in others. Government, business, and union administrators
must unite in their responsibility to so conduct themselves and
their organization that the aggressive impulses of people are
adequately sublimated in activities that unify rather than keep
them divided.

The pessimists declare that the impulses toward hostility
and destructiveness cannot be permanently rationally controlled. The hate impulses innate in the psychobiological en-
dowment of man can be renounced through sublimated
activity that, at best, brings only partial release and satisfaction.

This argument states that every culture is based upon com-
pulsory labor and instinctual renunciation. People must be
taught and forced to renounce their aggressive impulses by
putting them to work for productive purposes. The essential
task of the administrator thus becomes to see that the individual will want to do what he has to do, under the given organization and economic conditions. People must be helped
to enjoy what is inherently painful and uncomfortable and to
fear what is inherently pleasureful.

But because this is basically unsatisfying, the unexpressed
aggressive impulses every now and then break through to
threaten the controls set up for their peaceful expression. Each
act of rebellion is followed by feelings of guilt, which seek ex-
piation through further stronger renunciation of aggressive impulses. This act repeated over and over has resulted in the
paradox that organization, which was instituted to release

man's efforts, also binds him into a tighter and tighter straitjacket. The primitive always seeks to break out from within
the modern. The various elites, including administrators and
educators, may attempt to help the individual sublimate more
effectively, but, even so, the primitive will now and then pop
out to take charge only to be put back in under a stronger lock
and key.

From this point of view, war, rebellion, conflict, low morale,
unstable loyalty, and grave moods of depression and self-
indulgence are inevitable. The administrator must make life
tolerable, but he can never do enough. He must control those
impulses that now and then turn upon the instrumental power
that he wields. At best he can help to forestall the next rebellion, but unknowingly he only increases its eventual proportions.

The Optimistic View

The administrative problem concerns how to put power and
order to work effectively to channel aggressive impulses into
productive forms. Freud, a chief proponent of the pessimistic
view, believed man was his own worst enemy, trapped between
his instinctual demands and his prohibitions against their
satisfaction. Man was born to be neurotic.

Freud's biological and anthropological premises were subjected to widespread attack. Some charged that not man's
nature but society was responsible for his neurotic condition.
Freud accepted the traditional belief in a basic dichotomy
between man and society. Man to him was fundamentally antisocial and had to be checked and channeled by authority and
education. However, others replied that all human characteristics and emotions are products of social experience, and great
emphasis should be placed on learning to live. Neurotic and

destructive living is not biological heritage, but a product of social circumstances, pressures, and habits.

This theory allows a more creative and democratic approach to the problem of how to administer to the needs of people. It suggests that the executive must recognize the problems created by his role and strive to modify them. It suggests that his fall in the Great Depression can become the beginning of his usefulness to contrive social mechanisms that will allow better sublimation of aggressive energy into socially desirable and productive forms.

The optimistic view does not offer an easy solution. Neither the executive nor the people he controls are in a static, definable relationship to each other. The taboos, pressures, laws, and regulations against the use of the executive's instruments of power and order are seldom direct expressions of intent and feelings. The relationship is at base essentially ambiguous, based upon strong unconscious tendencies of hostility and distrust, camouflaged by respect and deference.

The executive will be increasingly guarded and guarded against, directly and indirectly. His solution lies in recognizing this growing ambivalence and putting it to work for his and their mutual needs. As he moves out into his society to assume increasing responsibility, he should be aware of the underlying hostility that may be occasioned by his attempt to become more useful. His increased power must be accompanied by increased sensitivity and responsibility or he will fail again.

We do not want to give the impression that our society is so organized that all people are totally dependent upon the administrator for the opportunity to act. However, in a managed society freedom will be found in organization if it is found at all. But may not everyone be expected to understand and practice the administrative skill? The executive at the top can do much to reorganize to meet the needs for participation and freedom. The welfare of society and of his business, government, or association rest largely upon the view the executive entertains of his role.

But there is just so much the executive can do himself for the many who are caught in the bureaucratic machinery. After all, no one can hand him his freedom on a silver platter. We have tried to show how many people inside and outside the organization impede and resist the executive's assumption of responsibility. The extent to which he will experience a sense of freedom and opportunity depends upon the extent to which he knows the art of administration.

The same condition holds for all members of a managed society. Whether in the home, school, church, or community, organization must be made to work for the cause of human freedom. Each individual must become skillful in dealing with administrators, in knowing their attitudes toward the public, and understanding their views of human nature.

President Kennedy was correct when he said that more than anything else, the executive's view of the executive role itself is crucial to how he intends to perform. The same may be said for both public and private administration. The public must become informed about the various views of the executive role. They must become skilled in assessing and interpreting administrative behavior, whether in public or private organizations. By this means they will become more able to participate intelligently in the determination of the conditions by which they are expected to be active and orderly.

In short, the extent to which members of a managed society excel in the art of administration or in the understanding of administrative behavior will determine their opportunity to exert genuine choice, experience a sense of freedom, and engage in shared planning and responsibility. Administrative skill or understanding is a prerequisite for each individual to achieve productive expression of his unique capacities. Without this skill and understanding, he will continue to exist in the same meaningless framework of well-ordered activity.

The optimistic view offers awareness of administrative practices as a desirable, if not necessary, objective for all. As every member becomes administratively skilled or sensitively aware, the suspicions and distrust toward administration will lessen. Not the least important will be the development of a set of expectations on the part of both administrators and non-administrators concerning their responsibilities and how they might be productively fulfilled. The ambivalence surrounding the executive role will be greatly decreased. Much is to be gained if each member of a managed society assumes intelligent responsibility for playing productive roles.

In conclusion, placing further restrictions on the executive must not be done without justifiable cause. No society can afford to tamper carelessly with the power and order necessary to achieve effective administration of their needs and wants. A wise and mature society dedicated to democratic values will support and respect those who assume the responsibility of administration and will be able to recognize that point at which autocratic and bureaucratic methods exceed administrative necessity and conflict with the democratic values of the society at large.

Our society is making serious, careful judgments about this question. It must determine if the means by which our society is organized are in harmony with the ends to which we are dedicated. But if it is confused, it is definitely not a sick society. It is a sick society that refuses to watch diligently the extent of this conflict between means of controlling people and the human values the society holds. We were that sick society during the era of the robber barons and captains of industry. While these titans abused their powers, neglected public welfare, and made a travesty of human rights, the public turned the other way expecting little else from profit-minded people. If the people had been stronger and more aware, they would not have allowed these inroads into freedom and human dignity. Unfortunately, the people blamed the titans and not their own inaction.

The rebellion that ensued was not the inevitable working of innate instinctual impulses. The optimistic view offers the possibility that the businessman's "fall" was due largely to a failure to appreciate the subtle signs of human deprivation and oppression. The failure lay in the attempt to control without recognizing that administration must consider basic human needs and emotions, including ambivalence toward administration itself. They failed to control by serving and serve by controlling. They failed to administer within the executive duality.

CHAPTER 3

EXECUTIVE CALISTHENICS

The executive's role is determined by the conscious and unconscious forces and needs in his society at any given time. However, in the actual performance of this role, the executive works with specific people in his environment who transmit and manifest these needs and strivings in specific forms. It is, of course, of fundamental importance for him to see the over-all picture which we discussed in the preceding chapters. But he is confronted with major problems needing immediate attention which may seem only distantly related to his emerging role in the total society. He serves his society mainly by serving the few people who actively draw upon his energy and attention. If his society is meaningfully represented to him, it is by and through these few people who make up his administrative unit. Consequently, whatever view he holds of the executive role will be most reliably seen in his pattern of behavior with those closest to him.

To begin this study of executive practices let us first note, somewhat belatedly perhaps, in the third chapter of a book on the executive, that the word *executive* means to follow (*sequi*) out (ex), as, for example, the executive branch of the government follows out the instructions of the legislature. This act, to follow out, presupposes both the recognition of authority and the assumption of authority. The executive is in a subordinate capacity to those above and in a superordinate capacity to those below, whom he may use to help carry out his responsibilities. He is above and also below; he receives and also gives; he orders and also obeys. The face he turns upward may not be the face he turns downward, and his side view may be a little bit of both.

The Executive Posture

The executive life is represented by this composite of emotional opposites. The executive both stands and crouches, dominates and submits. Each posture requires separate skills and calisthenics. He must know how, when, and whom to serve and control. The forces and needs that require these reactions do not always declare what mode of response is appropriate.

His upward relationships are typically viewed as relations of uncertainty. To carry out the orders of those above him without exerting some degree of influence on them places his own authority in jeopardy. To the extent that those above him are dependent upon him for carrying out their designs, he has opportunity to exert upward pressure.

Today the executive must respond to many forces of interest and authority. The chief executive in business, for example, must be responsive to his board of directors, stockholders, public opinion, market demands, governmental regulations, labor unions, and his own managerial personnel. These diverse interest and authority-granting groups often present most difficult problems with overlapping and inconsistent demands.

His posture must necessarily be flexible. He must be sensitive to the conflicting demands and alert to opportunities for resolving them.

As a servant of so many masters, he cannot help being an enemy of some of them. Each interest or authority-granting group sees its own problem and wants its own solution implemented. The executive is at the center of these demands, and may be the only one to recognize the conflicts and inconsistencies of the demands. No one else feels the pressure of the converging powerful forces, and because they do not occupy his central position, others often do not understand the basis for his decisions. Interest groups such as unions may exert strong opposition, and authority-granting groups such as boards may place restrictions upon his powers of control. Hence, these many masters are also to some extent his enemies.

The power of these masters confronts him. He moves away, then moves in, stands up, crouches over, takes a stand, loses an argument, bides his time, rushes into battle, but always seeking a favorable resolution of his dual role of dominating and submitting. Whatever solution is achieved, it is mercurial. He seldom achieves finality. There is always the possibility that his masters will change positions. They often move with changing circumstances that are marginal to the executive's viewpoint.

Thus, a union's concern with broad political trends may change its interpretation of the relation between labor and management in a particular firm. Financial trends in the stock market may change the director's views of budgets and expenditures. Overnight these forces may emerge or recede, always leaving the executive with the problem of what constitutes a proper response.

In this atmosphere of change and diversity, the natural response is to try to achieve certainty and consistency. The executive cannot help but strive to obviate the mercurial quality of his power and authority. He must control but he also must serve. But the problem upward and outward is matched by the problem downward and inward. The small scale of primitive society may have justified a harsh, superordinate show of strength and determination. With the rise of large, complex organization the superior is as dependent upon his subordinates as they are upon him.

He must fix authority on specific subordinates, lighten his own load of responsibility, engage in mutual discussion, and accept the expertese of his departmental representatives. He may choose his subordinates because they will make him look good or carry out his assignments with dispatch. But if they are strong, competent men they will exert countervailing influence just as he may in turn strive to soften the demands of his superiors. His dependence upon his subordinates becomes their advantage and his advantage is in their dependence upon him.

He can facilitate the discharge of their responsibilities and provide escape hatches for their dilemmas. But men of major duties and responsibilities tend to place great faith in their own perceptions of reality. The struggle to dominate is deeply ingrained in both their character and the system. In this interplay of upward and downward motions, an administrative balance emerges which is always precarious and volatile. He is in some ways both master and servant.

But achieving proper conduct toward members above and below in the organization is only part of the problem. This is the era of the team man. The executive's peer must also be considered. Although he may be outside the duality implied by a strict interpretation of the executive role, he cannot be ignored. The awesome fact for the executive is that he must include the peer in the problem of how, when, and whom to serve and control.

In the past he was concerned primarily with his upward relationships. The boss ruled as the monarch of all he surveyed. He kept every subordinate looking at him. They were not to turn left or right, because they needed no help or advice from each other. They were completely dependent upon him. Subordinates could be directed by arbitrary control. But as size and complexity, unionism, labor cost, and governmental controls increased, it became economically necessary to build good will among employees.

Gradually the subordinate executive or supervisor was allowed to acquire a face of his own. He substituted smiles and charm for directing by the seat of his pants. But he was only allowed to acquire a new downward face. The face he turned upward was still the same old one of dutiful respect and industriousness.

The executive life became more complex as the need to build good human relationships downward increased. A paternalistic attitude became common among supervisors. At the same time accusations became widespread that good human relations practices were simply used to manipulate and dominate the worker more effectively. In the growing confusion, top management, which had used subordinates as hirelings and clerks, became aware of the increasing need to delegate responsibilities and develop highly trained experts to then give advice. The human relations movement eventually spread upwards all the way to the top.

The strong iron hand was gloved in velvet. However, the subordinate executive was still largely directed and controlled.

But as decentralization and specialization increased, the boss became aware of his dependence upon the subordinate. Clear boundaries of authority and control were gradually blurred. How, when, and whom to serve and control became less matters of authority and more matters of judgment. The individual had to turn to himself.

To make matters more ambiguous, the peer became almost as important as the subordinate and the superior. He had to be consulted for his expertese and his essential support. No longer could the subordinate executive expect the boss to keep the peer in line. The peer acquired a face in his own right. Decisions were worked out in group or committee atmospheres. Although the boss often bossed, much of the information and deliberation that entered into his final decision became a collective affair. The support and good will of peers have become almost as important as those of subordinates and superiors.

The Lonely Executive

The growth of the importance of the peer has contributed to what may be called the peer orientation. Many chief executives tend to treat both subordinates and authority-granting groups as colleagues or peers. Consequently, the hierarchical orientation that had been so useful in telling when to sit or stand, thrust or parry, has become increasingly limited.

In some executives the peer orientation has tended to generalize the hierarchical orientation into a power orientation. The hierarchical orientation is useful in categorizing the power and authority that people hold. The modification of the hierarchical orientation by the peer orientation amounts to categorizing people in terms of their power without regard to their position in the hierarchy. The peer orientation combined with

the hierarchical orientation thus becomes an invaluable tool
for assessing what is important or irrelevant, when to tread
carefully or stride firmly.

However, the increasing acceptance of the peer orientation
tends to place the executive on his own even more. No longer
able to depend upon the easy formula of the hierarchical
orientation, he must meet each situation from above, below,
and the side as it is presented. It is seldom appreciated how
much the executive today must rely upon himself to formulate
the correct response. Although he is in the midst of teeming
numbers of people, he actually must stand on his own feet. He
is alone and lonely. Many speak glibly of the other-directed
executive—guided by a radar set fastened to his head, continuously telling him what others below, above, and at his side
expect of him. Thus, the motives and directions of the other-
directed executive stem from others. He is able to respond,
but not to choose; he has no effective center of motivation of
his own.

However, this individual, who is presumably other-directed,
could not make an effective executive unless he possessed a
mechanism to filter out the irrelevant information that bom-
bards him from without. To be sure, the executive today must
be more sensitive to what is going on outside than his predecessors were. Executive communicating has become more
subtle and indirect. Cues are becoming important ways
whereby executives relate to each other. Where the executive
chooses to be indirect, cues are intended to mean more than
they appear to mean. For example, to express dislike for an
idea the executive may not always degrade the idea; he may
ask to think about it for a while. To warn a subordinate, he
may avoid him temporarily; to show his sense of priority, he

may practice the art of strategic omission. Rather than dismiss an idea coldly, he may contribute a better one; to avoid a touchy subject, he may interrupt insistently. And, of course, there is the executive who remarks, "very interesting," to an idea because he fails to understand it or chooses not to reveal his doubt. One superior cues his subordinates by looking or talking to the ceiling whenever he wants to appear objective. In another case, a president is accustomed to show his antagonism by being overly polite.

Thus, executive talk must often be simultaneously translated into two languages—the apparent and the intended. The former serves as the vehicle for the latter. Being indirect is justified by convenience and efficiency. Many things can be said better by innuendo. Some things said directly would cause undue anxiety and lowered morale.

Probably the most important result of the subtle approach is that it forces the executive to develop his powers of observation and interpretation. These qualities are important because, as the executive moves to the top, the area widens where superiors inform without actually using words and subordinates act without actually being told. To develop sensitivity the executive must have a creative flair for the unspoken word and the ambiguous sentence.

There are some who sense in this growing tendency toward purposeful ambiguity a tendency to avoid committing oneself unnecessarily. No doubt this motive is prevalent. However, one must not fail to realize that the executive world is populated with people on the right and left, above and below, wherein team work is at a premium. Executives have to live with each other in closely related activities that have torn down the aloof formality of the autocratic past. In such a team atmosphere,

care and consideration of others are extremely important. Tact
and caution in place of their predecessors' objective arbitrariness are functionally contributions to effective administration.
The more other-directed the executive becomes, the more he
must rely upon his own capacity to detect and interpret what
to do, when, and with whom. If he mistakenly zigs when he
should zag, he may not know it until it is too late, and the
consequences may be almost irrevocable.

With the growth of the peer orientation, authority and
power become increasingly subtle and indirect. Yet the executive must be just as responsive to these suggestions as if they
were commands. The peer orientation may allow him to
present a more consistent face to those above, below, and at
the side, but inwardly he must make interpretations involving
greater risk than in the past when he merely had to turn the
one, proper face upward. Today he must stand alone.

The Search for a Formula

No formula exists to tell the executive how to conduct himself among superiors, subordinates, and peers. Nor can a safe
one be easily found. In spite of his desire to seek a comprehensive solution to establish his position for all times, his
strategy must necessarily be forged within the acceptance of
ambiguity. His behavior must be guided by two taskmasters—
external and internal reality.

The executive must be keenly aware of the external forces
acting upon him, their motivations and their demands. But he
must also be responsive to his own inner dynamics. To dominate or submit, to decide or advise, to accept or reject, all
command the attention of strong impulses within his personality. These impulses to dominate and submit must be fused

into a unified pattern of effective action. When reality requires domination, he must not submit. If submission is required, he must control his aggressive drives to dominate. Often a mixture of both is required, at which time a delicate mastery of these aggressive or submissive impulses must be effected.

The executive lives in a high pressure system wherein the consequences of lack of emotional control are frustrating and often catastrophic. Few can consistently meet the requirements of reality with the proper administrative and emotional responses. The ensuing external conflict is often caused by a struggle within. The executive cannot avoid the consequences of oversubmission or overaggression. Never adequately mastering others or himself, he cannot take leave of the battle, seeking, struggling, holding out hope for eventual victory of some kind.

For many the need to achieve a stable, permanent resolution of these problems of the executive role becomes the major mode of response (see Chapter 8). Other executives, of course, reveal in their experiences an easy acceptance of these ambiguities and never seem to be overwhelmed by them. However, in counseling situations where they needn't be quite the master that others think they are, they, too, may show a rather extensive pattern centered around continual difficulty with resolving the problem of when, how, and whom to control and serve.

Within both government and business, when to dominate and submit is a problem of crucial importance. A look at some of the people who have held the highest positions shows that few achieve a reliable formula that tells them what to do and when. Most executives experience a continual struggle within and without. Success seems to be found in having a good batting average.

The American Presidency

The American presidency may be used to illustrate the problem of knowing when to serve or control, withdraw or advance, parry or thrust. Consistency fails.

A former Roosevelt aide once wrote that cabinet officers safely forget half the president's orders. The president is told that the problem is being investigated if he chances to ask a second time. If he asks a third time, a wise cabinet officer will give him at least a part of what he wants. But only rarely and about the most important matters, do presidents ever get around to asking three times.

One can literally wear out his effectiveness by assuming a primal, superordinate position on all affairs. A case in point is Eisenhower, who in many respects arrived at the presidency with an immature mechanism for knowing how, when, and whom to control or serve. Neustadt relates that before the heat of the 1952 campaign, President Truman accurately reported that Eisenhower's problems as president would be, "He'll sit here and he'll say, 'Do this! Do that!' and nothing will happen. Poor Ike—it won't be a bit like the Army. He'll find it very frustrating." Eisenhower evidently found it so, remarks Neustadt. He quotes Robert Donovan, "In the face of the continuing dissidence and disunity, the President sometimes simply exploded with exasperation."

As late as 1958 an Eisenhower aide reported to Neustadt that the president still had not made a satisfactory adjustment to the problem of when to parry and when to thrust. "The President still feels that when he's decided something, that ought to be the end of it . . . and when it bounces back undone or done wrong, he tends to react with shocked surprise."[1]

[1] Richard E. Neustadt, *Presidential Power*, Wiley, 1960.

Naturally all men explode once in a while when dealing with problems involving huge risks and stakes. Even the most experienced executive may under these circumstances regress to the clumsy use of authority. The consequences may be even more tragic because the opponent is afforded insight into one's sensitive areas. Others will then jump in and make the matter worse. Eisenhower, for example, showed unusual restraint all through his administrative career with such problems as the provocation by Egypt's Nasser and Cuba's Castro and the Red Chinese shelling of Formosan outposts. When McCarthy attacked him personally, Eisenhower again showed unusual restraint by relying upon public opinion and the efforts of his friends in the Senate to deal with this gross misconduct.

But on one problem he showed the autocratic style to "eat out" insubordinates. And from then on the president had torrents of gripes and challenges fall his way. One of his ablest and most loyal supporters on Capitol Hill, Senator Styles Bridges, tried to tell Eisenhower about his concern for the weakness of the national defense program. Alsop described the president as turning crimson, then white, with fury and launching into a volcanic tirade against the presumptuous persons who dared to suggest that such weaknesses exist.[2] On this subject Eisenhower repeatedly lost his composure toward those who dared to challenge his opinion. He vented his displeasure on overly independent and outspoken military administrators and several left the service under high pressure from the president. Many used his rigidity as an excuse to leave, to stay, or react strongly.

In each of these unrestrained occasions the president showed the "quick, hot flash, then the whiteness of the jaw,

[2] Joseph Alsop, "The Eisenhower Puzzle," *New York Tribune*, May 18, 1960.

and then the spate of angry words." What he accomplished with this unusual lack of restraint is not known, but it is evident that many of the Pentagon brass who were inclined not to stick their necks out became acutely responsive to this higher pressure. Those who stayed were brought into line; many others might not have had to leave if the president had attempted to bring them into line with more oblique or subtle approaches.

The president, however, seemed to want to stand up and be counted on this issue. But on this issue he should have sat and listened. Much of the criticism he received from the military and Congressmen for his directed verdicts concerning the defense budget only ruffled him further. Because he chose to move against these criticisms rather than with them, his successor, Kennedy, made splendid political capital out of them during the 1960 election. In this instance Eisenhower seemingly failed to realize that his powers of authority and prestige were most effective when placed in the service of the administrative needs and purposes of conscientious subordinates who depended upon him for help and guidance. Not even the president can arbitrarily command without serving the needs of those commanded.

Eisenhower always seemed to be a prisoner of his own staff. He delegated his authority to Sherman Adams, who in turn came to dominate the president to the point that when he said "we" he often meant "the President." When Adams came under criticism for accepting gifts, Eisenhower said, "There is one man I do need." Sherman Adams ruled for several years as an autocrat who seemed to know the workings of the presidency far better than the president himself. Under Adams the White House took on the character of an independent center of power, most notably illustrated in the dumping of Joseph

W. Martin from his position as minority leader in the House in 1959.[3]

Dulles and Humphrey dominated the president on foreign and fiscal issues. He tended to place a great deal of trust in experts on issues in which he had little background or interest. The president was often forced into uncomfortable positions with his own subordinates because he could not make up his mind whether an issue was for his consideration or for theirs.

The U-2 incident was a gross error not only politically but administratively.[4] When the Russian premier announced that an American plane had been shot down over Russian soil, spokesmen for the state department and the National Aeronautics and Space Agency agreed that it must have been a weather plane operating from a base in Turkey. The pilot had lost consciousness owing to some failure in his oxygen supply, and the automatic device that took over moved that craft off its regular course.

Then Khrushchev shook the administration with the announcement that the pilot was alive and kicking 1200 miles within Russia with his spy equipment equally intact. Secretary Herter made an embarrassing announcement that the plane probably was on a reconnaissance mission, without authorization, however. After a weekend of dreadful worry, the nation was next informed that Eisenhower had authorized the flights and they had been going on for several years. Herter affirmed that the government would be derelict in its duties if it did not take such measures to safeguard against another surprise attack. Vice President Nixon next appeared on a New York television program and affirmed that the United States should

---

[3] See Clinton Rossiter, *The American Presidency*, Harcourt, Brace, 1960, p. 169.

[4] See Ernest R. May, *The Ultimate Decision*, Braziller, 1960, pp. 230–234.

not cease to assume its responsibility to maintain its welfare simply because a plane had been shot down.

Finally, on the following day Eisenhower, who still had not made up his mind whether to zig or to zag, decided that the flights would be discontinued and reversed in spirit and fact his secretary of state and vice-president. It is now apparent that Eisenhower did not act quickly enough to prevent others from committing gross errors of administrative judgment. But he could not very well instruct others in administrative propriety if he did not himself have and show good judgment. It seems in reversing Nixon and Herter he admitted that we were spying; the first time such an admission had ever been made in modern history.

Eisenhower just could not immerse himself sufficiently in the on-going stream of administrative problems to sense adequately what was going on. If he zigged when he should have zagged, he also did neither much too often. His lack of timely response at times bordered on administrative anarchy.

Truman is often pictured as a strong, decisive executive who seemingly had no trouble in determining who should decide or be served. However, this "Man of Independence" continually struggled with this problem. Truman remarked about the powers of the president, "I sit here all day trying to persuade people to do the things they ought to have sense enough to do without my persuading them." There were times when Truman showed great independence of judgment. There were also examples of unusual acts of reliance upon others. One of these occasions was the Marshall Plan.

Neustadt reports the scene well.[5] In a commencement address at Harvard in June, 1947, Secretary of State Marshall launched what Truman later accepted as the beginnings of

[5] See Neustadt, *op. cit.*, pp. 54–60.

the Marshall Plan, the European recovery program of 1948. Eight months before Marshall spoke at Harvard, Truman's party lost control of both houses of Congress and two weeks before Marshall's speech Truman had vetoed two prized accomplishments of the Republican majority, the Taft-Hartley Act and tax reduction. Yet scarcely ten months later the Marshall Plan was under way, having cleared the obstacle of a traditionally isolationist congressional leadership intent upon economy.

How this amazing feat of cooperative effort was accomplished is too lengthy to relate. The major feature was Truman's amazing sensitivity in knowing how to trust, depend upon, use, and move with the people crucially involved. He merged with Marshall, Vandenberg, Stimson, and Patterson. But although he relied upon them, he also exerted strategic control. He seemingly served and controlled at exactly the proper times on this occasion.

On other deals he seldom achieved this splendid blending of the duality of the executive role. His forced reversal by the Supreme Court on the government's taking over the steel mills was surpassed only by his continued hesitancy to put MacArthur in his place. Since the outbreak of the Korean War MacArthur had overstepped his bounds as a subordinate to the commander-in-chief. Truman showed considerable vexation at times, but nevertheless went along with him. In August of 1950 he considered firing the general, but by October he had calmed down to state that MacArthur was loyal to the government and to the president. "There is no disagreement between General MacArthur and myself." Truman actually invited MacArthur's final act of insubordination by tolerating a long series of such acts. But, when the general publicized a demand for enemy surrender on March 24, 1951, Truman fired him for insubordination. He showed little mastery here. But the mistake had been made many months before when he chose to submit to or remain silent about MacArthur's aggressive onslaught rather than to dominate him.

Few knew how to be the total master of the immediate administrative situation as well as Franklin Roosevelt. He seemed to know when to say the right thing, give in, let others talk, be accommodating, issue strong command, and blast his opponents off their Congressional shelves. He seemed to sense innately the strong reactions of authority figures and governmental officials to his dominating influence. He knew well how the state department, treasury, and the military could sustain fantastic degrees of inaccessibility and inconvincibility. To change anything in these areas was like punching a feather bed. "You punch it with your right and you punch it with your left until you are finally exhausted, and then you find the damn bed just as it was before you started punching." Roosevelt, however, seemed to know where the bed was weakest and jabbed away with infinite luck and success.

But even this master of the art of dominating and submitting made some bad mistakes. He almost committed vulgar primal acts when he arbitrarily rode roughshod over Congress. He lost much influence by such poorly devised programs as packing the Supreme Court. In 1937 Roosevelt lost patience with the Supreme Court which had handed down decisions invalidating some of the emergency legislation passed in 1933. In his attempt to add two justices, the attitude, "They can't do that to me," was only thinly disguised by an insincere concern for the "health" of the "nine old men" and making provision for their retirement on full pay. Roosevelt lost the court fight, the ensuing attempt to "purge" the Democratic

Congress, and his party incurred severe losses in the 1938 congressional election.

He was saved from this incredible affront by an equally incredible mistake on the part of the Republicans in 1939. Instead of being thrown out of office in 1940, he went on to win his unprecedented election because the Republicans, under the leadership of Senator Borah of Idaho, refused to modify the Neutrality Act on the ground that there would be no war. If there was a war, the GOP would be politically bankrupt on the eve of the 1940 presidential election, and that is precisely what happened when Hitler's army streamed across the banks of the Rhine in 1939.[6]

In spite of these errors, Roosevelt seemed to possess a sensitive mechanism for knowing just how far to go before he would have to reverse himself. When this capacity is not fully developed, the executive will frequently be outmaneuvered and humiliated. Although Churchill had great presence in most situations, among the giants he seemed to lack the finer sensitivity of where and how to make his stands. He often failed to prevent the future possibility of having to back down.

For example, during the preparation to attack Europe, Churchill decided that he should go aboard the supporting naval ships in order to witness the attack by the Allies on the beaches of Normandy. Although he did not have to consult Eisenhower, whose authority did not include administrative control over the British organization, he was nevertheless refused by him. Before a showdown could develop, aid came to Eisenhower from an unexpected source. The king heard of Churchill's intention and informed him that if he felt disposed to go on the hazardous expedition, he, the king, felt

[6] See John F. Carter, *Power and Persuasion*, Duell, Sloan and Pearce, 1960, pp. 160–162.

it to be equally his duty and privilege to be at the head of his troops. Eisenhower wrote, "This instantly placed a different light upon the matter and I heard no more of it."

During the European campaign Eisenhower reported several difficult situations with Churchill, mostly due to the latter's inability to seek or accept advice. When Churchill had to back down, it was always with considerable reluctance. Montgomery reported that he made erratic decisions to the point of catastrophe. Churchill suffered at times from inability to manage satisfactorily the problem of when to zig or zag.

In the presence of the master, Roosevelt, Churchill never had much of a chance to dominate. His psychological equipment was not keen enough to show him where he was heading and how to avoid a humiliating demise. One minor example concerns the conference at Teheran where, as usual, Roosevelt was seeking to gain supremacy over his other two conferees, Stalin and Churchill. To do this he manipulated by holding occasional meetings with Stalin from which Churchill was excluded. To ingratiate himself further with Stalin, Roosevelt began making fun of Churchill. Lifting his hand to cover a whisper, Roosevelt said, "Winston is cranky this morning, he got up on the wrong side of bed." Stalin began to beam, whereupon Roosevelt began to tease Churchill about his Britishness, about John Bull, about his cigar, about his eccentric habits.

The more Churchill got red and scowled, the more Stalin smiled until finally he broke out in a deep, hearty guffaw. Both Stalin and Roosevelt allowed mild sadism to gain its momentary release with Churchill the victim. The latter could not see through the thinly veiled acts of needling. In more serious situations he seemed unaware of the subtle maneuvering going on around him. This crimp in his perceptual equipment may have contributed to his inability to stand or to crouch, dominate or submit at the proper times.

The Inflexible Policeman

The consequences may be grave when the executive fails to make the proper response. An executive may spend his entire career trying to establish a system to relieve himself of deciding what response is proper. The patterns followed to obviate this problem of when, how, and whom to control or serve are infinitely complex and they may grow topsy-turvy without systematic curtailment.

One of these patterns, known as an "independent jag," consists of liquidating opposition. But although the opposition seems eliminated, deep wounds are left which may break open under the slightest pressure. One false step may start a sequence of heavy reversals that may leave the executive without support. The habit of independence breeds the inability to be submissive. All previously acquired support may disintegrate as a result of one improper move.

This is illustrated by former Police Commissioner Stephen P. Kennedy of New York City. In the attempt to remove petty graft and loafing as a drain on efficiency, Kennedy set up rules and regulations that he supervised personally when he took office. He swept aside the dead wood, shunted recalcitrants, moved and removed at will those who were not amenable to his authority. His subordinates were punished first and investigated later.

Civilian complaints were swiftly acted upon even though they later turned out to be malicious and unfounded. The commissioner used both individual and mass transfers as disciplinary weapons. At a single stroke he once transferred every sergeant who had served more than five years in one precinct.

In a four month period he moved one-fourth of the sergeants in the department. He was the complete master of under-over relationships. He dominated to the point of dictatorship. Kennedy made the 24,000-man police force into one of the finest in the world, for which he received lavish praise. But he left deep wounds. Several incidents compounded at the right moment brought a storm of controversy that erupted into rebellion.

One of these incidents centered around his objectively unjustifiable command that policemen relinquish all secondary jobs. The policemen claimed that they had to hold other jobs to survive economically, that the secondary source of income helped to keep policemen honest and above petty graft, and in addition, that firemen were allowed to hold these jobs while policemen were not. Because of the objective verifiability of the policemen's argument, Kennedy found his Cromwellian Ironsides had turned to papier mâché. And he retaliated to hold his men in line. He never saw the need to parry; he thrusted away to near oblivion. Unequivocal discharge of some, probation of others, and transfer of many, including the head of the Patrolman's Benevolent Association, upset the whole police force. The control that had been first used to achieve constructive results was now met by wholesale rebellion.

The whole system of discipline began to fall apart, first with aggressive action on the part of the patrolmen in issuing violation tickets to the public. Two and three hundred percent more tickets were issued (which oddly enough cut accidents and deaths drastically). Furthermore, the patrolmen indirectly threatened to call a "sick strike" on election day, for which Kennedy set up a corps of volunteer physicians to examine any man reporting sick. To reshuffle his force again in order to regain discipline Kennedy resorted to assigning policemen to higher duties without promoting them. This was a willful violation of a state Supreme Court ruling against such assignment of men, and the Court threatened to jail the commissioner if it happened again.

Although the commissioner knew when he took the job that he was not entering a popularity contest, his rise and sudden fall revealed more than this truth. Essentially, he too often zigged when he should have zagged. He set a firm course, but failed to see the danger signs. His case points out that although support may appear to be strong, it is inherently unstable and may quickly collapse. Yet, although it may be perishable and volatile, support from above and below is the prerequisite for executive performance and the executive must seek it.

But to seek support he must also give support. To gain power he must yield to power. Whatever gains the executive makes must be plowed back into his performance. Whatever he takes must be returned. In short, whatever power he acquires must be put into the service of those from whom it is taken. To do otherwise is to violate the character of the executive role.

Sensitive Flexibility

This fact must be a decisive ingredient in the executive's view of effective performance of his role. Any executive act is aimed at doing something with people who are above him, below, at his side, or outside of his company, government, or association. People tend to want to control those whom they serve and to serve those who control them. The effectiveness of the executive is found within this duality. He controls by serving and serves by controlling. His opportunity to act is always conditional.

The conditionality of the executive role prescribes that there is no set formula to determine reliably how, when, and whom to serve and control. The executive must be sensitive to the events that unfold upon the administrative scene and prepare action tailored to their particular character. In short, he must be flexible enough to respond to his perceptions of different situations.

Stephen P. Kennedy was not flexible enough to sustain crucial support from the policemen. Truman was insensitively flexible with MacArthur. Roosevelt moved with insensitive rigidity against the Supreme Court and then attempted to purge Congress, but was saved from his court-packing fiasco because the Republican party failed to seize the proper initiative. If the party had moved to take advantage of the situation, history might have been substantially different.

Any individual is capable of only limited flexibility, because he has only a finite set of responses to deal with the infinite demands and pressures that bombard the executive responsibility. No administrative problem repeats itself. Yet the executive finds himself performing routine activities from day to day. Flexibility is called for in the rare cases of exceptional circumstances. How these few crucial occasions and major problems are handled largely determines the executive's overall success.

Some people display little flexibility on these occasions. Crises may bring out their intensive desire to control by overwhelming. They may display autocratic tendencies. Others may feel the need to seek others to share in a deliberate approach to the problem. They may display democratic tendencies. Still others may set up a system to handle all known major problems and those which cannot be anticipated. They may show a bureaucratic tendency. Although all executives are dependent upon a system of well-regulated effort and all perform routine functions, it is their handling of major problems that gives us insight into their view of the executive role. In such cases they may be led by their own dictates, seek group advice, or depend largely upon the policies, precedents, and practices of the system.

In many cases the executive style manifested in the major problems may be different from the style used to handle everyday problems. Autocrats of detail sometimes become the bureaucrats of crisis. Group decisions are sometimes more relied upon for policy matters and autocratic commands for interim assignments. In addition, elements of the three styles exist within every individual and characteristics of all three styles will be displayed over a period of time. This can be considered a normal deviation from the normal. In such cases he may be expected to be subject to change without notice. Consequently, many executives appear flexible because they display a wide range of behavior in handling routine assignments, as opposed to major or crucial problems, and because they display varied patterns of emotional reactions. The executive who remains rigidly the same, always predictable, is less likely to make compatible and responsive approaches to new and different problems.

How, when, and whom to serve or control becomes determined by habit rather than reality. The executive will zig because he never tried to zag, or because zagging at one time failed to achieve intended effect. In a society as dynamic as ours, where change is the only constant, a well-proportioned administrative mix, seasoned carefully by ingredients from all three styles, is needed. A single-ingredient administrative style is an anachronism.

However, the proper amalgam is not clear. So much depends upon the individual and his particular administrative situation. What is clear, however, is that each executive must diligently practice assuming administrative responsibility with refreshed insight and vigor. He must deliberately practice crouching over, standing up, thrusting, and parrying. These executive calisthenics will gradually enlarge his range of flexibility. And the basis of this practice must be a broad view of the executive role.

President Kennedy was right in asserting that the executive's view of his role is more crucial in determining his behavior than his understanding of particular problems. However, the executive must have a realistic view of the role. No executive may loom forth in gigantic proportions to dominate unilaterally the events and people that surround the administrative role. The effective executive is sensitively flexible so as to both serve by controlling and control by serving. Executive life today is represented by this composite of emotional opposites.

CHAPTER 4

HOW EXECUTIVES DEVELOP

The executive faces the never-ending task of knowing how to command and accept command, to dominate and submit, to give and take. He does not bring to this responsibility a clear mandate from within whereby he can serve and control as the situation presents itself to him. He is not inwardly a zero. Rather he brings to the situation experiences, abilities, and needs that determine how he will deal with these complex problems. He must act in ways responsive to his own inner forces and needs and cannot simply bend whichever way the administrative situation warrants even if his future career depends upon it.

Facing the responsibility of knowing how, when, and whom to serve and control is not really new to him. All his life he has been attempting to solve problems of knowing when to stand up or sit down, talk or listen, dominate or submit. Executive calisthenics are blown up exercises in childhood manners and morals. A basic problem of the child is how to live and grow in a world dominated by powerful adult figures. On the one hand he needs their support; on the other hand he wants to be free

of them. He must serve them, but wants to control them. How
the infant extricates himself from this basic duality determines
to a great extent the inner forces that will control his behavior
as an adult in performing the executive role. The point is he
never really does extricate himself entirely. Because of certain
experiences in his past, he may choose the executive role. Or
the particular responsibility of the executive role may repel
him and he may seek another form of expression for his needs
and ambitions.

The individual who aspires and successfully assumes the
executive role may approach it from three crucial positions,
any one of which may become dominant and all of which are to
some degree imbedded in his childhood experiences. He may
approach executive responsibility by aiming to achieve a position of power that minimizes the need to be subjected to the
strong, aggressive interests of others above, below, and at his
side. This is the autocratic response. A second approach results
from the desire to protect oneself from the central ambiguity
of the executive role by a system that determines for the executive how, when, and whom to serve and control. This is the
bureaucratic response. The third way is to recognize and respect the interests and pressures for what they are and engage
in shared administrative responsibility. This is the democratic
response.

Conditions as potentially ambiguous and uncertain as those
that bombard the executive may turn his aggressive energy
inward in the service of the self, restrain his energy by the
sacred adoption of rules and regulations, or release his energy
outward in the service of others. Power, order, and love are the
basic themes of response to conditions of uncertainty. We
shall be concerned with these three responses as they pertain

to the problem of performing within the bounds of the executive role.

The Power Impulse

The autocrat has a strong desire to thrust himself into the breach and to overwhelm by overresponding. Action becomes the essential mode of response. For the autocrat, the greatest feelings of confidence, strength, and mental vigor result from pitting himself aggressively against his adversaries who may intend to move him in directions contrary to his will.

Power is largely but not exclusively represented in the autocrat's response to the executive responsibility. What accounts for his tendency to seek power is not well understood. One prominent view starts with recognizing that birth itself is the most arbitrary of all experiences. The fetus is pivoted inside the warm lining of the mother's womb into a position of ejection into the cold, unstructured world. The first experience at birth is a spanking to dislodge waste matter from the vital lung and oral regions. He is arbitrarily fed, clothed, cleansed, and attended to by big, powerful adults over whom he has no control. Later he comes to see these powerful adults in terms of the advantages and satisfaction they provide.

Presumably, the power impulse develops out of growing awareness of how power differentials may be used to restrict him. The child usually passes through a stage in which he prematurely attempts to reduce the power gap between himself and his parents and other adults by asserting the power impulse. He usually experiences just enough success and failure to strengthen this impulse in his developing character. The power impulse may become modified by the affiliative impulses, that is, desire to love and establish close relationships, but there is always a residue of the power impulse. Thus, it is seen that the duality facing the executive is in some ways similar to the duality facing the infant. He is ushered into an ambiguous condition of need for more powerful figures and desire to control them.

One explanation of the development of the power impulse is "The Legend of Our Lost Omnipotence." This theory suggests that as an infant the individual experiences himself as the center of the universe. He is powerful and mighty. His parents are not seen as powerful, but rather as servants who jump to his every cry and need. Wanting seems to bring perfect satisfaction. Later, just wanting proves inadequate and the habit of being served causes the child to develop the use of gestures and words to have his wishes fulfilled. Then cries, tantrums, shaking, and eventually hostile, hateful tendencies become expressed to acquire the necessary satisfactions.

As the blurred figures become faces and figures, the child becomes aware for the first time of intentional deprivation. To be deprived is one thing, but to become aware that his servants willfully deprive him of what seem to be his rightful possessions and satisfactions is a traumatic experience. The world that was his to command becomes filled with powerful adults who are immune to his outbursts of cries and anger. Not only do these crude creatures withhold satisfaction, but they also impose their will.

Struggling to uphold his omnipotence, he is gradually defeated and the awful, ambiguous duality begins to emerge. He must learn to be dominated and yet he strongly wants to dominate. He learns to accept their control because of the advantages, but he wants rather their power. In short, the child becomes aware of his need for parents, but he also resents their control over him. But when he begins to become accustomed to this combination, he begins to be pushed away from them. He is "in the way," "a big baby," "a mother's boy." For some reason or other people do not want him around. He becomes afraid and resentful, but gradually adapts to the requirements of having to seek his own support from those with whom he might live, play, and later study and work.

In the conflicting swirl of ambiguity, the child eventually seeks to develop resources of his own that will be true to his needs and wishes in contrast to the fickle loyalties of his friends and parents. The power impulse is born out of the need to achieve once again the certainty of that omnipotent time of infancy. Some individuals attempt to resolve all ambiguity by becoming submissive rather than dominating. But submission may be only another expression of the power impulse, for one may control others by being useful to them as well as by using them. Although the dominating and submissive reactions are present to some extent in every adult, some individuals are motivated chiefly by the impulse to dominate.

The Oedipal phase of growth cycle seems particularly crucial in resolving the problems of how and when to dominate and submit. The child is positively conditioned by his parents as they minister to his pleasures, and therefore he has varying degrees of love for them. However, he may come to hate either one of them for monopolizing the other's attention which might be beneficial to his own love needs. The development of these love-hate reactions reaches a climax when the boy comes to want to possess his mother and remove his father. The father is seen as his chief rival for the mother's love, and as a rival he is a potential source of danger and harm.

This fear of the father not only produces hostility toward him, but also induces a repression of the desire for the mother. The fear, which is actually a realization that the father is more

powerful, gradually is replaced by identification of the child
with his father. He begins to incorporate characteristics of his
father into his own personality and gradually acquires a picture
of the person he himself wants to become. But becoming a
personality independent of his parental and substitutive authority figures increases tension and feelings of guilt. Char-
acteristically rebellious tendencies are always attached to
specific acts of obedience and conformity. The unacknowl-
edged feelings of hostility actually break out at times, to be
followed by guilt reactions of submissiveness and deference.

Ideally some satisfactory resolution occurs whereby the
ambivalence is no longer consciously felt. This is achieved by
costly renunciation and repression of powerful hate impulses
and their sublimation in the form of productive and morally
proper goals and activities. But these unconscious feelings of
hostility are always operating, however silently.

The tendency to give active expression to the hate impulse
is stronger in some than in others. In a few individuals the
need to be hostile and destructive is so strong that it seeks
expression in acts of violence and physical combat. In others
it becomes diverted into socially desirable and acceptable
forms. It may take on the form of competitiveness and striving
for success and wealth. The hate impulse may lead others into
activities where they can dominate and control other people's
activities. And it is these individuals who become executives
with behavior centered on the power impulse.

The Hierarchical Orientation

Every society has escape mechanisms which induce but
never fully allow the sublimation of the power impulses. In
particular, formal positions of authority offer opportunities to
channel these strong impulses into productive forms of en-

deavor. The individual within whom these power impulses are strong may use this opportunity to dominate the affairs of his subordinates and actively strive to be useful so that he will become indispensable to his superiors above. He will attempt to so serve and control that he will achieve mastery and power over others. In short, he will put his strong aggressive impulses to work within the aims of the administrative role. His attempt to exert one-man control places him squarely in the autocratic style. In such executives a hierarchical orientation is at work. It is often called "bicycle psychology" because of the position of the rider who is bent over (submissive above) with feet trampling down (dominating).

The hierarchical orientation gives the executive the disposition necessary to achieve instrumental use of people. Ruling from above he can gain the necessary aloofness and mobility to employ his men with dispatch and precision. He achieves control through distance and impersonality. He avoids entangling human problems that harass those who allow themselves to become attached to subordinates. At the same time, the autocrat's bicycle psychology allows him to show the necessary obedience to perform diligently in the service of higher authority. He is responsive upward. This factor in his administrative format is often misunderstood.

Autocracy means self rule or one-man control. The element of bowing to others above, looking to them for orders and support, seems to be contrary to the meaning of one-man control. However, the power impulse is often productively expressed by the attempt to gain support from others above so that the subordinate can rule over and for them. Although the autocrat may strive to accomplish this, he may have to settle for something less. Whatever the case, he is at his productive best when he is able to so follow the dictates and needs of authority-granting powers above that he becomes essential to their activities. He controls by becoming indispensable. His indispensability provides his independence. In his attachment to them he acquires his separateness. He is both below and above his superiors.

Of course, there are some who are intractable. They cannot control their emotions enough to accommodate this strategy to achieve one-man control. The productive type of autocrat may be contrasted with the bully who is not capable of maneuvering people into a position of dependence. He wants to, but he cannot. He feels most intensely the ambiguity of needing to serve by controlling and control by serving, but somehow he cannot muster the necessary restraint to perform diligently within this duality.

In some cases the bully is not sufficiently aware of the necessity for organized activity. He is not aware that freedom and independence are always conditional and accrue from the ability to serve and support others. The productive autocrat's administrative style is derived from the ability to control people above him by overwhelming them with his competence, skill, and loyalty. He puts himself completely at their disposal, and when successful he is given wide latitude. However, the bully becomes a threat and consequently seldom achieves that degree of latitude or freedom needed to pursue his own choices.

The toady also fails to acquire the degree of independence needed to perform in the autocratic style. He submerges his personality completely, does all that is expected of him, and never makes demands upon himself. He rids himself of all responsibility, doing exactly what he is told.

The productive form of autocracy is found in striving to find opportunity and authority to make independent choices concerning the use of power. This means that there must be some initiation of activity through personal choice on behalf of the superior's interests and authority. Both the bully and the toady lack this attribute in their behavior with superiors and consequently may not succeed as well in hierarchical structures.

The hierarchical orientation common to all autocrats represents a basis of dealing with the problem of how, when, and whom to serve and control. The productive autocrat accepts the duality of having to serve and control and makes it the vehicle for his administrative format. It is the key to his view of his executive role. But he does not succumb to the duality. He puts it to work for him by incorporating it into his basic responsibility. The productive autocrat is distinct from the bully who cannot accept the duality even enough to use it to dominate the authorities who serve as objects of his hostility and from the toady who succumbs to the duality and does nothing about it.

The autocrat who achieves maximum effectiveness within the executive duality is one who accepts superior authority as given and who controls it with his competence, skill, and personality. His major instrument for achieving this control above are his subordinates below. He serves upward by controlling downward.

The face he turns downward requires more careful scrutiny. This is the better known face of the autocrat, for it registers the more common meaning of autocracy. He tries to make himself the key to all relevant activity going on above or below. In practice, he affirms that his first responsibility is to maintain his authority and power. He does not attempt to protect his authority by a withholding pattern. He is a man of action who maintains through doing. (The downward face of the autocrat is so interesting and crucial to our understanding that this aspect of autocracy will be dealt with more thoroughly in Chapter 5.)

The Order Impulse

The bureaucrat is the methodical man who cannot meet the demands of the executive's ambiguous responsibility head on and mold them to fit his personality, but rather he muffles them in the intricate passages of his administrative format.

He is intent on maintaining and perfecting the system. He serves others by serving the system; he controls others by controlling the system. The system stands between him and all others, whether superiors, subordinates, or peers. Nothing stands between the autocrat and those whom he controls or serves. The dutiful face he turns upward and the demanding face he turns downward are unmediated. The bureaucrat, however, always shows the same face, whose minor changes in expression reflect only the different demands of the system. In this sense the bureaucratic response appears to come closer to resolving the executive duality by first recognizing that the inherent problem of how, when, and whom to serve and control is dependent upon what set of rules are to be followed.

The autocrat plays the game by placing himself and his subordinates in the complete service of superior authority. When this is done up and down the line a hierarchy develops with increasing degrees of authority and power toward the top. What holds the layers together is obedience and loyalty to the superior. In bureaucracy personal authority and force are replaced in the relationships of superior and subordinate by internalized rigid rules and regulations. The system becomes the integrator of human energy and will.

The bureaucrat, therefore, plays the game differently. The

anchorages of his duality are not the same. Whereas the autocrat wants to identify with and incorporate the authority and
power of his superiors, the bureaucrat wants to identify with
and incorporate the power and authority of the system. By
serving the system he serves the boss, because the boss is as
much a part of the system as the subordinate. One might say
that they have the system in common. They both must learn
how to operate within the confines of the bureaucracy.

The bureaucratic executive must anchor himself to the system, but he must remain sufficiently aloof from it to master
and control it. He, too, is always torn between standing and
sitting, fighting and listening. Both his chief friend and worthy
opponent is the system which at any time may be represented
by his superior, peer, or subordinate.

The Putting-In Tendency

In practice the bureaucrat becomes an expert who occupies
a precise niche in his organization or society. He surrounds
himself with instruments of expertese that rely heavily upon
trained and specialized abilities. Some refer to his condition as
trained incapacity.

The base of the bureaucratic impulse is the acceptance of
being bounded by technical expertese. The individual consciously or unconsciously strives for maximum effectiveness
within a limited activity. In other words, he takes on limited
definitions of himself. He is not a doctor but a pediatrician,
not an executive but a comptroller. He pours his aspirations
into narrowly prescribed roles that afford reliable and precise
channeling of his efforts. The narrower the role, the better
understood are the requirements to achieve proficiency. He
becomes in mind and temperament what the role prescribes.

This need to put oneself in a bounded, limited role or activity is crucial to the act of accepting the life of an expert. Strong deposits in the personality feed this "putting-in" complex. Many of the adult's strongest emotional experiences are anchored within bounded areas. For that matter, it is natural to all living things to grow within some bounded area. Bears live in caves, bees in honeycombs, and ants in sandy hills. Life is conducted by first being restricted. Random behavior of the newly born becomes gradually systematic through activity within confined circumstances. There is just so much that can be done within an egg shell, for example, but what is done is made possible because of the orderly and efficient arrangement of the necessary conditions and resources for the purpose at hand.

Human life itself spans the emergence from a womb to incorporation into a tomb. The fetus is lodged comfortably in a protective layer of warm throbbing tissue and liquid. After his ejection into the cold, unbounded world swaddling clothes, folded arms, soft caresses, and warm breasts are provided to engulf the infant to help him recover the feeling of confinement in the accommodating womb. Life and reality later take on increasing meaning within the bounded areas of cribs, rooms, homes, yards, buildings, offices, bureaus, organizations, communities, and states.

To the growing child the home becomes a labyrinth of rooms in which specialized activities occur to the exclusion of others. One of these rooms is the toilet wherein he must learn to put his waste material into a chamber. Later, he is taught that knives go in one bin, forks in a second, and spoons in a third. If a girl becomes threatened, she puts herself or her doll in a closet or bureau away from would be assassins or kidnappers. If a boy becomes frightened he hides in garages or under steps. He is later taught to put money in toy banks, food in refrigerators, clothes in closets, jewelry in strong boxes. As the child grows older he learns that garages are for cars, living rooms for strangers, recreation rooms for fun, kitchens for eating, and bedrooms for sleeping.

In all of this training in the home, the child acquires an unconscious view of life as bounded or circumscribed. He never really believes that he is free to become anything and everything. This is a myth he entertains only in dreams and imagination. His most profound experiences occur within bounded areas and unconsciously he comes to use these experiences as a way of dealing with reality and himself. The putting-in complex allows him to seek out confined activities and roles. In our organized society this ability and desire is a basic mechanism for achieving productive expression of his needs and capacities. It allows him to seek specialized training, to become an expert.

The unconscious desire to become bounded enables the factory worker to put his personality into a restricted job or task and become identified with it. Without the putting-in tendency, man could not be moved into the narrow roles found in our society, except by force from external authorities or by strong push from within.

To some it may seem incredible that modern man is capable of living eight hours a day in a factory or office performing extremely limited functions of a routine, systematic nature. No doubt this capacity is born partly of both power and affiliative motives. It is made possible also because human development necessarily occurs within structures that offer convenience and comfort. In this sense, the adult never really leaves home. Wherever he goes he tends to make it his home. He finds within any area of confinement a way to give expression to his needs and interests. He uses his restrictive conditions as a way to express his personality.

Whereas the putting-in tendency is the necessary condition for acceptance of a fundamentally bounded pattern of behavior, by itself it tells us only that every one is bureaucratic to some extent. It does little to explain why some are more bureaucratic than others to the extent that they may be properly called "bureaucrats."

The bureaucrat is marked by an inability to tolerate unbounded or ambiguous circumstances or events. Rather than making him easily upset and erratic, this intolerance for ambiguity contributes to his controlled, disciplined, and proper behavior. A tendency to be overcontrolled may be partly due to the means by which he deals with his strong, aggressive impulses. The putting-in impulse arises from a reaction to the destructive impulses. Because these hostile impulses are feared and distrusted, they must be regimented. The bureaucratic type puts himself in a straitjacket that will ensure proper, efficient, and moral behavior.

A most important phase in childhood is the transition from infantile megalomania to the experience of the profound ambiguities of responsibility and control. This period is known as the anal stage, and it is generally during this stage in the child's development that toilet training is begun. He has achieved sphincter control by this time, and the erogenous zones around the anal regions are particularly sensitive to variations in temperature and pressure. The child then faces a complex problem. He wants to derive maximum pleasure from the act of defecation and to maintain his uninhibited gratification of this physical need. However, this gratification is opposed by parental demands for regularity and cleanliness. Also, the child soon learns that he will win praise and approval from his parents if he submits to their demands. His infantile megalomania feeds on physical gratification, but it also demands praise, so the parents' praise and the pride the child derives from it can to some extent be substituted for physical gratification. Each successful act of sitting on the seat of the closet and the resulting praise add to his feelings of being an important and unique person. He will become pretentious, arrogant, despite what others have, and take pleasure in sole possession. He develops parsimony. To establish some control over his parents, while submitting to their authority, he insists on choosing the time and place for evacuation. So strongly may he preserve his right of decision that he may sit on the seat of the closet until exasperated parents remove him and then let go with total defecation. He must control them somehow.

In the adult the anal impulse may develop into the qualities of perfectionism, retentiveness, and obstinacy. The anal type will hold to his own system or habits, be thorough, accurate, orderly, and regular. He will enjoy putting himself into a routine set of sequences such as getting up every day at the same time, going through the same sequence of toilet habits, and eating breakfast as systematically. At work he will put himself in at eight and out at five, only to put himself back in another bounded area or function at home.

His perfectionism and obstinacy may be expressed in the belief that no one else can do things quite as well as he and that no one else can be relied upon to do them properly. Because he wants to be correct and thorough he may become quite expert in some areas. In these areas he sets high, rigid standards of performance to which he adheres conscientiously and meticulously. These rules, regulations, and standards act as boundaries to his alternatives of choice and decision. He resists any invasion of his bounded area of proficiency. In this way the anal traits reinforce the general life pattern of becoming comfortable, secure, and productive within bounded areas and functions.

The bureaucratic response entertains ambiguities as intense as those of the autocratic respones. Some who want to put themselves into the arms of the system may lack the inner controls necessary to stay sufficiently aloof at the same time. This individual may at times rebel in bullish ways and refuse to go along with the system, even risking the possibility of being ejected by it (see the discussion of the "bu-reaction, pp. 192–194). Because he may become an object of threat to those who rely upon the system, he may actually intensify the ambiguity of life in the bureaucracy by drawing attention to the problem itself. When the bully stands outside of the system and shouts, he can be dealt with effectively only by withdrawing the advantages the system has for him. This practically spells personal ruin for the rebel, since the advantages of the bureaucracy are so great today.

The other extreme response to the bureacuracy is the conformist. One must live in bureaucracy but not overwhelmed by it. Some executives submerge themselves in the bureaucracy so that the system rules them. They exert little countervailing influence and take all their cues from the needs and regulations of the bureaucracy. The conformist thus overcomes the uncertainty and doubt of how, when, and whom to serve and control.

Both the rebel and the conformist pay a high emotional cost to live in organization. The power impulses are wasted or inhibited rather than used productively. The productive use of the power impulses is the essence of the effective solution of the problem of how to serve and control. Autocracy and bureaucracy are basically power impulses. The bureaucratic style centers on order and becomes expressed primarily in a systematic orientation. The autocratic style centers on authority and becomes expressed in a hierarchical orientation. The bureaucrat becomes marked by his capacity for caution, the autocrat for quickness; the one for efficiency and retentiveness, the other for action. The bureaucrat attempts to find power in order, the autocrat power in authority.

The Sharing Impulse

The democratic style is based on the affiliative or love impulses. As an executive, the democrat affirms the norm of sharing. In this respect he is the natural enemy of the autocrat. Autocracy means rule by one, a monopoly of power and authority. Democracy means rule by the people, a diffusion and sharing of power and authority.

Autocracy restricts subordinates; democracy releases them. The autocrat demands unconditional obedience; the democrat offers unconditional respect. The autocrat makes decisions alone; the democrat deliberates with others whose interests are involved. The autocrat feels compelled to move out and above the group; the democrat wants to live in and work through the group. No two views could be as dissimilar as to what constitutes the proper role of the executive.

However, both autocrat and democrat must act responsibly within their administrative frameworks. This means both must control. One can now see that the ambiguities in the meaning of autocracy, bureaucracy, and democracy have confusing consequences and produce new problems as soon as the relations of the three concepts to each other are considered. Autocracy and democracy are often contrasted in such a way that democracy is identified with a resignation of power and autocracy with a denial of love. The contrast between powerless love and loveless power is unavoidable if power is identified as something bad and love as something emotional.

The prevailing stereotype of the executive is a man at the center of a communication network, receiving information, weighing probabilities, and making rational decisions with vigor, dispatch, and precision. Every stereotype, of course, contains some truth. But this one ignores the executive as an emotional, affiliative being. For some reason the executive is often viewed as a powerful, orderly person who either is not capable of love or rejects this capacity in his business life.

Fundamentally, the mistake is viewing love as sympathy and display of affection. These may be acts of kindness, but they do not constitute the basic condition of love. Love, a rational activity of the ego, is a condition of relating to reality. It is foremost a capacity to share oneself. The individual shares his knowledge, skills, ideas, and beliefs with others who need them. Love is the active helping of others and as such constitutes a vital quality of the executive role.

Without this concept of sharing, the ambiguous term of democracy cannot be made explicit. Autocracy is the monopolizing of power, which in practice divides the superior from his subordinates and peers. Democracy is the sharing of power, which in practice unites the superior with his subordinates and peers. In autocracy the superior and subordinate act as two; in democracy they act as one. Thus, the individual and the group are given administrative relevance when power and love are viewed as legitimate administrative qualities. However, unless the prevailing stereotype of the executive is enlarged, there is no way to account for democracy in his administrative scene.

In fact, democracy is seldom seen as a legitimate administrative responsibility. In the past the executive had no choice but to project a view of himself as a powerful and orderly unit of action centrally located at an intersection of oncoming demands and pressures. We have pointed out in Chapter 2 why this image was entertained. Although more executives are today giving attention to the democratic style, it is perhaps not because they are committed to democracy. More executives try out democracy than have the democratic commitment, and few have a clear understanding of what administrative democracy is. If one were to point out to the typical executive that genuine administrative democracy is predicated on the capacity to share oneself with others, the reaction would be one of profound doubt or disagreement, owing largely to the fact that this view has heretofore been alien to them.

The problem crucial to the democratic style concerns the need to help people help themselves. Freedom is as tricky and volatile to handle as power. It is not something that can be granted, and freedom without ability to use it effectively may be returned in the form of overly rebellious or submissive tendencies. In this respect, the democratic style can produce much the same reaction as the autocratic style. Sometimes those subordinates who know least about using their freedom productively may raise the loudest voice for freedom. Similarly, those who seem best equipped to exert independence of judgment may seek the comfortable security of domination from above.

Whereas there are many who would misuse and abuse democracy, modern organization inherently sets narrow limits upon the extent to which the executive can encourage freedom among subordinates. The prevalent hierarchical and systematic functions impose restraints upon the democrat so that he seldom has the freedom needed to encourage freedom in others. Torn between his strong desire to affirm freedom and his constant fear of its misuse and abuse, he is confronted with an ambiguity as intense as that felt by the autocrat and bureaucrat.

The forces that bombard him are as whimsical, volatile, and ambiguous as any that inhere in the executive role. He can be one day a genius and the next day a jerk, loved and then hated, approved and then restrained. To perform effectively he must know how, when, and whom to control and serve. Those who would abuse freedom must be treated differently than those who would misuse it. The face he turns to some may not be the face he turns to others. He may dominate when he should submit, zig when he should zag. The necessary procedures and the relevant consequences seldom declare themselves on their own accord. He must interpret without sufficient cues, he must risk, and he will make terrible mistakes. The consequences of his errors may be more threatening than the errors of the autocrat and bureaucrat, because democracy develops late in character formation. If it does become a part of the personality, it is often tenuously anchored.

The democrat cannot achieve an easy resolution of the ambiguity of his role. He may be prepared inwardly to share, but be compelled outwardly to withhold. He typically constrains and restricts more than his ideal self will allow. Invariably the democrat has a much greater difficulty than the autocrat in being himself and being administratively effective.

The democratic style is not rooted in power. The executive does not manipulate the other person, but shows respect and responsibility for him and the desire to help him become a fully useful member of the organization. The democrat moves toward rather than against people. How this capacity to share develops is indeed as difficult to understand as the other two impulses of power and order. A favorite view suggests that the basic condition is a high degree of loving and being loved as the child passes through those turbulent and potentially neurotic stages of ambivalence and ambiguity. Theoretically, sharing arises from a desire to overcome the anxiety of being both dependent and independent, unified and separated, accepted and rejected. In other words, sharing is an act of trying to unite productively with others.

The act of birth is a separation from oneness with the mother. The estranged circumstance attending life is contrary to physical need. The infant cannot stand alone. He needs others first to nourish him and later, when he becomes acutely aware of his essential separateness, to reunite him.

This reuniting is a crucial act, however. The mother shares herself freely and unconditionally with the growing child. At first he accepts her love on the basis of his needs. By being loved unconditionally, he learns to feel secure and wanted. The father's love is conditional upon the son's identification with the father's characteristics and facilities, those capabilities the child will need to make his way in life. Obedience to the father becomes the basic virtue and the punishment for disobedience becomes withdrawal of fatherly instruction and concern. Whereas mother has the function of making him feel secure, the father has the function of making him productive. The one provides the basis of feeling at one with others, the other provides the base of being productive with others.[1]

This is accomplished by parental sharing of affection, understanding, knowledge, and resources. Because they share with the child, he learns to share in return. At first his basic narcissism does not allow him to share himself without expectation of return. But during adolescence his narcissistic impulses become

[1] See Erich Fromm, *The Art of Loving*, Harper, 1956.

modified by genuine object choices. He begins to love and associate with others for altruistic purposes. He steadily comes to accept people and their motives for what they are. Because he has the capacity to share himself freely with others, he has the capacity to overcome his essential separateness. But while becoming associated, he does not destroy the separate identity of those with whom he associates. He does not engulf or destroy by his loving.

A gradual resolution of the Oedipus ambivalence is at work. He is becoming a person in his own right. He sees himself as free and separated in that he has his own future to realize, his own life to live. However, he is united with his parents because he has the capacity to share his affection and understanding. He is both a respectful son and a free person. In turn, while seeing them as his parents, he relates to them as a free person. He has successfully mastered the authorities of his past.

Now he is able to meet with his peers and employers on the basis of their unique qualities. If he dominates, it is not because he is still trying to surpass his father or possess his mother, but because inwardly he seeks to realize his true abilities and skills. If he submits, it is not because he has been overly dominated by authority figures, but because he wants to acknowledge the needs and motives of others for what they are. The love impulse modifies the hostile impulses to make them productive and socially effective.

Sharing means giving one's knowledge, skill, beliefs, to others who are in need of them. The act of sharing is marked by an interest in the needs of others without expectation of return in kind. The giver sends his very best. The ideal of sharing is to help another individual become fully ambulatory by means of his own resources. This kind of sharing leaves the superior and subordinate stronger because the superior is provided the satisfaction of being useful and the subordinate acquires new skills and opportunities. Their separate identities have been preserved while they unite under common banners. They grow together in different ways because of different need satisfactions.

Ideally the superior works himself into a position of high superfluousness. His skills and abilities elicit and develop skills and abilities in his subordinate that disallow his continued control. A peer relationship arises that forces into the background many of the hierarchical differentials. The newly acquired skills belong to the individual and are not systematized into formal procedures and regulations. They remain personal and individual, as the superior gives the subordinate opportunities to find his own ways of becoming more effective. In this way the superior does not make his subordinate into a carbon copy of himself. Nor is his skill or routine generalized arbitrarily into a system to which all give deference and loyalty. The autocrat's technique of smothering and the bureaucrat's technique of engulfing are confronted by the democrat's technique of releasing the unique qualities of others.

In the sharing orientation the needs of the other person become the basis of sharing oneself. The conflicting requests, pressures, and commands that bombard the executive are responded to on the basis of their objective needs and purposes. Both individual and organizational needs are always involved. When the two are mutual the problem may not be insurmountable. When the individual's needs conflict with the needs of the organization, it may be almost impossible to reach a satisfactory resolution. Nevertheless, the needs of others become the basis of the democrat's response.

Consequently, his face upwards is marked by a basic willing-

ness to respond to the objective needs of the organization. He
is not overwhelmed by the opportunity to serve, does not use
such opportunity as a basis for advancing his interests above
those of others. He does not desire to use subordinates and
superiors to his own advantage. He is just as apt to protect
his subordinates from irrational demands from above as he is
to protect his superior's interests in the activities of his own
people. The arbiter is to what extent these demands above and
below are related to the good of the organization, which is
common to both subordinates and superiors.

He does not attempt to become indispensable. His greatest
interest is strengthening his superior's hand rather than engulfing him with aggressive acts of deference, loyalty, and
enterprise. Ideally he fears no one, the strong or the weak, is
not willing to be shoved or bribed, and resents the show and
use of threat. He practices persuasion with the affiliative
rather than the coercive or expertese touch. And his persuasive
talents are as much at work in his superior's interests as in his
subordinate's. He will argue, debate, and seek to convert his
boss when he feels that he is wrong and improper. Furthermore, he is offended when superiors make decisions about his
subordinate's interests without his consultation. He will fight
arbitrariness and rudeness from above with as much vigor as
the autocrat fights resistance from below. He is repelled by
acts of human indignity and disrespect.

The impulse to be democratic may be so tenuously ingrained that the executive cannot tolerate antidemocratic
views and behavior in others and he will impose his need to
be democratic upon others. He forces them to conform to his
pattern. This executive is democratic to the point of being
autocratic. He shares himself with others only when they will

practice sharing themselves with him. If they are nice, he is nice; if they are responsive, he is responsive. When they are not kind, he is nasty; when they are not helpful, he is not helpful. He may be called a "democratur," for he enforces his democratic style with autocratic means (see pp. 227–228). In the name of love the democratur seeks power and order.

The democratur seems to be common today. Wanting to share but not able to tolerate the ambiguity that is inevitably involved, he is never sure what to do. The democratur may sit when he should stand, talk when he should listen, thrust when he should parry. In the interest of democracy he may seek to know of people's problems, but at the same time he may use people, restrict, and deny, all because he knows better what they need than they do. He appears to share, but he is not capable of sharing without guarantee of return in kind.

His human relationships are marked by a bargaining quality. What he does is to exchange himself with others. He gives in order to receive, praises in order to be praised, loves in order to be loved. He attempts to make his superior look good so that his superior can make him look good. The approval he seeks from below is also expected from above. When this technique fails, he will enforce it with all of the power of his position and personality.

Others in whom the capacity to share is precariously back-stopped may tend to depend too much on the group. Here there is no bartering. The individual is completely anchored in the group to the point that he cannot resist its values and pressures. He seeks to share so that he becomes shared by others. The conflicting pressures that bombard the executive role are transferred to the group for resolution. The groupist thrives on standing, permanent committees, which he chairs as conference leader. His task is to help them bring to him agreed-upon decisions which he then can take to those whose interests may be affected.

With the group solidly behind him, the groupist attempts to be responsive to the responsibilities of the executive role. While submerged in the group, he feels little the ambiguity of the executive duality. He stands and sits as the group so wishes and decides. He takes all of his cues from them and relies upon their infinite wisdom. While other executives today cringe and take to their battle stations at the sight of oncoming thrusts by interest and authority groups, he merely diverts them into the lap of the proper committees. The groupist acts as traffic cop who sends cars in the proper direction, keeping the streets free of congestion.

The mature democrat may use commitees too, but it is not because he wishes to escape from the executive duality. He recognizes that someone must give direction and control. He does so through a capacity to share his knowledge, skills, and affection that is born of strength rather than feelings of weakness.

The Antisocial View

We have observed that, for the most part, meaningful and altruistic sharing comes late in the development of the individual. For many it is only precariously anchored in the personality system. The sharing orientation is an ideal which few actually attain.

The sharing orientation represents transformation from selfishness into love. In religious themes, love for mankind is often taken as the norm for the human life. But this religious ideal is accomplished only by God and his representative, which for Christians is Jesus Christ. Because God, who sacrificed his Son for man's inherent sinfulness, is the only true representation of love, this norm is put beyond the reach of the rest of the human race. Consequently, on one side is God and love and on the other side is man immersed in self-gratification. The dilemma is found in the requirement to love mankind, which itself is sinful and unclean and unworthy of the love of God. The struggle to love that which is not love is an ambiguity from which only a few, the saintly, achieve extrication through Divine Grace, mediated through faith, the sacraments, and the saving works of Christ.

Freud also believed in the limited capacity of man to be weaned from his narcissism. All have a primal instinct for death and destruction. Paralleling this hate instinct is the sex instinct which, taken by itself, is constructive and affiliative in social relationships. Together the hate and love instincts may fuse so that the most benign human relations, such as philanthropy, become at best mere sublimations or by-products of sex and aggression.

To Freud man is basically antisocial. He believed that the first father was an autocrat who ruled because he was the most powerful and could enforce his power. By means of prohibitions this first autocrat directed the destructive energies of the sons toward constructive ends. But the son rebelled and killed the tyrant, only to find that life without father was threatening to those who remained. To keep their destructive impulses from devouring each other, they renounced instinctive gratification. They forced themselves into a cultural straitjacket of rules and regulations which, in turn, held them morally and socially responsible.

Freud thought that men stand today as a band of brothers only because they have become accustomed to renouncing their true intentions of self-gratification. They are all basically

primitive autocrats who struggle to achieve the authority and
power of the primal father. But, of course, they cannot because
primal power is taboo (see Chapter 2). At best they can sublimate their power impulses into socially approved forms.
They may dominate by implementing the interests of the
group or, to put it more precisely, they may control by serving
and serve by controlling. The basic duality is inescapable.

The Social View

The capacity to relate to people as persons rather than
imagoes is for most not entirely possible. Consistent altruism
is a rarity. However, this may not be a condition of some primal
sin as the religious themes suggest or a primal insinct as the
Freudians suggest. It may be because of cultural pressures and
child-rearing practices. This view suggests that rather than
being at base an autocrat, the child is really a democrat, who
becomes warped by the patterns of his immature, tyrannical
parents. Therefore, although for different reasons, this view
essentially agrees that few have the capacity to share altruis-
tically.

In the womb, says the social view, the mode of life is
symbiotic in that the association relationship rules supreme.
There is no evidence whatsoever of destructive instincts. After
birth the association relationship in nursing, playing, and resting still remains dominant. The child is an oozing bundle of
positive affirmations of his total environment. As he grows
older he may make mistakes, offend, and receive punishment,
but he does not know they are mistakes until they have been
terminated by hostile acts of punishing parents.

The child learns at the proverbial mother's knee to hate and
engulf, destroy and tear apart, not because he is instinctively
hostile but because his desire to affirm his environment posi-

tively is frustrated. When his love motives are rebuffed, he learns to develop defenses which later become basic instruments for dealing with others. Thus hatred develops from love rebuffed. Although love may be the natural impulse, few emerge from childhood capable of sustaining for any length of time a wide span of shared relationships.

Erich Fromm goes so far as to suggest that the characteristic feature of our society today is the disintegration of the love impulse. He writes, "Modern man has transformed himself into a commodity; he experiences his life energy as an investment with which he should make the highest profit, considering his position and the situation of the personality market."[2] To Fromm the individual's aim is the profitable exchange of his skills, knowledge, and himself, his "personality package," with others who are equally intent on a fair and profitable exchange. "Life has no goal except the one to move, no principle except the one of fair exchange, no satisfaction except the one to consume."

The Struggle Within

The love impulse is certainly challenged by the cultural emphasis on success and achievement, the necessity of proving oneself, increasing standardization, manipulation of public opinion through propaganda, difficulty of identification with society and government, anonymity of big organizations, institutionalization of charity as found in the "drives" of the big national foundations and fund raising associations. Children brought up in such a milieu cannot be expected to transcend it. They adopt for the most part the character of their parents and superiors who are themselves struggling to get ahead, achieve, succeed.

[2] See Erich Fromm, *Man for Himself*, Rinehart, 1947, pp. 50–117.

However, our culture is not characterized by one exclusive social pattern. In opposition to these autocratic responses are many democratic ones such as the emphasis on charity, protective attitudes toward the weak, restraint of the strong, equalitarian relationships between children and parents, readiness to criticize governmental and parental authorities, tendency to accept others regardless of birth, mobility of the lower classes, freedom to dissent, emphasis on science, and rationality and readiness to accept ambiguity and conflict.

No one has a wholly consistent pattern of power and love, hostility and affiliation. Often the American is compassionate and forgiving, friendly and loyal, idealistic and religious. On the other hand, he may often be smug, indifferent, submissive, self-righteous, dominating, and downright repulsive. Consequently, personalities do not fall neatly into the categories of power, order, and love or their administrative counterparts of autocracy, bureaucracy, and democracy.

The struggle between the potentially antagonistic forces characterizes not only our present civilization, but every single individual. The fact remains that if only a few are saints, only a few are also representative of the other extreme. Only a few are unblemished democrats, only a few are total autocrats. Most are a mixture of all three.

Counseling with executives suggests that the impulses of power, order, and love are in continual competition within the individual. The internal autocrat declares war; the internal bureaucrat sets up the rules and conditions for battle; the internal democrat retaliates with love and understanding. The inner battle continues until one element is strong enough to bring about a cessation of open war. But the conflict goes on because power strives to become total and love cannot relax until power is permanently restrained. Because the bureaucrat will hear none of this talk about renewing the battle, the auto-crat and democrat continue the conflict by sly evasion, con-stant pressure, satire, humor, and wit. They evade the bureau-cratic censorship through elaborate concealment, but the con-flict keeps the bureaucrat disturbed and alert. Hoping someday to catch the censor unawares, the autocrat maintains an un-relenting pressure through the most devious means. The demo-crat is always forced to keep himself armed with the weapons of rationality and understanding. The peaceful compromise on the surface is more apparent than real.

For some, the battle within rages so bitterly and incon-clusively that all of the energy is consumed in an effort to reduce it. These are the neurotics who cannot live with am-biguity and must turn all of their attention to resolving it. They seek a comprehensive solution (see the discussion of the neurocrat in Chapter 8).

It seems reasonable to assume that young adults enter the administrative career with one of these three impulses becom-ing dominant. As they enter junior administrative positions in organizations early successes and failures help to establish the emerging impulse and provide a basis of fusion with the other two. Their experiences will be such that few will come through the administrative jungle without being more of one executive style and a little of the other two. Some may start out in one direction and because of difficulty change to an-other. These individuals may show an administrative career pattern of change to adjust to crises. On the other hand, some seem to arrive at the top with the same basic ingredients in their executive style as in the junior levels. Then, too, when some retire to a more passive life or change roles radically they may show a different aspect of their character.

Andrew Carnegie was a first-class autocrat as long as he

owned Carnegie Steel and served as its monarch. The bully became known as Saint Andy after he retired. Many have disparaged his desire to give away his millions and see his philanthropy as guilt. This may not always be the case. The executive role is such that even the most firmly anchored personalities become twisted away from their lifelong moorings.

Who would have guessed that the timid, seemingly hesitant personality of Lincoln could have moved with the autocratic vigor required to issue the Emancipation Proclamation? Who would have guessed that the strong, decisive General Grant would become an uninspired, unresponsive president?

Wilson was going to play the democratic role of being generally responsive to Congress, but when he became president and saw what problems were involved he accepted the role of enlarging the powers of the office. Wilson, who possessed a temperament akin to that of a shepherd guarding his flock, set forth the view that the president is at liberty in law and conscience to be as big a man as he can.

The office tends to change a man once he is given the responsibility. Cleveland was certainly not a man of dictatorial temperament. Yet in office he performed many autocratic acts, including numerous vetoes of congressional legislation and his singularly arbitrary command to the army over the protest of the Governor of Illinois to clear the way for trains carrying mail to Chicago. Eisenhower, whose skill at coordination brought the Allies through the war, became the head of one of our most uncoordinated administrations. The fumbling in the U-2 incident was not solely the result of a gangling governmental bureaucracy incapable of moving concertedly in a crisis. Too often when a firm hand was needed it was gently wrapping up another problem.

Contrary to the current arguments to be this or that kind

of executive, the typical executive cannot change that easily, except under extreme pressure. By the time he arrives at or near the top he is firmly anchored in lifelong administrative experiences and habits that prevent him from turning on and off at will the autocrat, bureaucrat, and democrat within him. The office may bend him away from a previous pattern of behavior only because his capacity and interest permit it. No doubt some are more capable of bending than others.

In conclusion, the problem of when, how, and whom to serve or control is not freely nor easily determined. The executive has two harsh taskmasters. They are himself and his organization; his inner needs and forces and those of the people he must deal with. To control others he must serve himself; to serve others he must control himself.

CHAPTER 5

THE AUTOCRAT

The autocrat represents a basic behavior pattern that is rich with tradition. Respect for power is an essential aspect of a healthy society. Our basic institutions were established in such a way that power rested with specific individuals who were expected to wield and guard it carefully.

This is illustrated by the presidency, which is an autocratic rather than democratic office and may be contrasted with the British cabinet which is based on the principle that the body is one in policy and responsibility. Each cabinet member, even the prime minister, is subordinate to the group as a whole without sacrifice of the energetic right to aggressive persuasion.

The American system is based on the principle that one man is responsible and his opinions are to dominate the administration.[1] Our past history has been dominated by men of strong autocratic tendencies. The parent, minister, teacher, doctor, and lawyer were all expected to be strong, decisive, domineering men. The men of power at the turn of the century so dominated their environments that businesses were

[1] See Herman Finer, *The Presidency*, University of Chicago, 1960.

identified with their single owners or officers. Newspapers were the personal voices of the editors and publishers. Thus *The New York World* stood for Joseph Pulitzer, the *Louisville Courier* was Henry Watterson. Colleges were linked with the names of their presidents—Harvard was Charles W. Eliot, Princeton was Woodrow Wilson, and Columbia was Nicholas Murray Butler.[2]

Business was largely autocratic with authority and power the major instruments of control. It still is not a representative institution, for executives are appointed from above, not elected from below, and participation has been historically accepted for purposes of collective achievement, not for representation.

Unions are largely the creation of great, powerful men of the past who followed distinctly autocratic patterns in their administrative behavior. According to material found by the Fund for the Republic, in most American unions the president is still all-powerful. The attempt to check his power by executive boards has not been too meaningful. Crucial to union democracy is the ultimate authority that rests with the convention. Although most unions nominate and elect officers at conventions, most conventions are kept well in tow by the union administration and its salaried staff, or "porkchoppers." Much of the president's power is derived from his authority to appoint convention committees in some cases or to preside over the convention in others. The concentration of executive power in unions has been rivaled only by that of business and government.[3]

The tendency to acquire independence, success, the neces-

[2] See Crawford Greenewalt, *The Uncommon Man*, McGraw-Hill, 1959, p. 20.
[3] See Leo Bromwich, "How Democratic Are Unions?" Fund for the Republic, reviewed in *Business Week*, July 25, 1959, pp. 111–112.

sity of providing oneself, to establish social distance to those
allegedly below on the scale of accomplishments and status,
contribute to the adherence of autocratic values.

The Problem of Rigid Categorizing

It is often noted that communal achievement necessitates
division of labor, restricting and ordering of motives and
efforts. Elaborate titles of prestige and distinction may be
given the men who move into the center of authority and control. However, they are seldom called autocrats, but rather
mayors, businessmen, educators, librarians, public servants.
Their styles or patterns of behavior are rarely understood by
the public. Only the effects are felt or discerned. If things go
along smoothly these men may escape close scrutiny entirely,
and when things do go badly they may not receive objective
analysis. Emotions flare up and whatever firmness they previously showed is interpreted in terms of the emotional demands of the hostile or frightened public. In times of social
and economic crisis, the mayor or businessman may be called
dictator.

Few words are as emotionally loaded as the word autocrat.
It is not a descriptive term for some people. However, to wield
authority effectively and not be autocratic in some ways is a
rare accomplishment. So much does the typical executive depend upon certain autocratic skills for his effectiveness that
it is impossible to describe his role and responsibility without
looking carefully and objectively at the total autocratic con-
figuration. To do otherwise would be to ignore what many
executives consider their major source of effectiveness.

The autocrat, bureaucrat, and democrat exist in precise and
separate forms only on paper and in the imagination. All executives are autocratic to some degree, just as all people have

some autocratic tendencies. It is not uncommon to find an autocratic business executive playing what seems to be a more democratic role in his home. It is not unusual to see a man exert arbitrary administrative pressure but personally conduct himself democratically. Roosevelt was himself a sensitive person, who many times went out of his way to salve wounded egos and restore lost pride. However, he knew how to organize people into the right combinations to keep them subservient to his wishes and needs.

Eisenhower's most outstanding public quality was perhaps charm, yet privately he ruled his household like a martinet. Mamie never knew in advance when he would blow his stack. Whereas Roosevelt wanted the White House maids and employees to be out in the open, conducting themselves as their duties demanded, Eisenhower never wanted them seen nor heard. It is interesting that Roosevelt rather than Eisenhower is often called the dictator.

It is questionable whether any one of these three styles is useful in describing a man's total life pattern. As we have mentioned, Andrew Carnegie seemed to be a ruthless autocrat who used others for his own ends. Yet, after he retired from business, he became "St. Andy," the great benefactor. He was, however, an autocrat, that is, his men at Carnegie Steel, Frick and Schwab in particular, knew and treated him as an autocrat.

The times at which one will be autocratic, bureaucratic, democratic are often quite predictable. Man is a creature of habit. He responds to his problems in ways that were successful in the past. Some problems may call for a behavior pattern that is not called for by other problems. Consequently, one may define his administrative problem in the home differently than his administrative problem at work. It is possible that he could emerge as autocratic in one context and democratic in the other.

Although Hitler and Churchill were completely different personality types with different ideological and political views, they did have one quality in common—"presence," that is, strong personal dominance and magnetism. These two historical figures believed in something greater than themselves. Their feelings of pride, self-esteem, and importance were committed to and fulfilled in the pursuit of their programs. This total commitment gave them the energy and endurance to see things through to their ultimate consequences, in spite of opposition. When they walked into a conference or meeting, people knew that they were men with whom they must deal.

No man is quite as strong as the one whose self-image is totally affirmed by the program for which he stands. His very presence forces others to ask themselves consciously or unconsciously, "Do I believe in myself as much as he obviously believes in himself?" It is in moments of truth like this that one is likely to discover the commanding presence of another.

These two completely different historical figures dominated and weighed heavily upon the minds of others. They were unquestionably the masters, whatever the atmosphere. No one dared pursue a topic of conversation that did not meet with their approval. Few dared to ask any questions or take any liberties. The British often found royalty easier to deal with than Churchill; the Germans often found the proud, rigid Prussian prince easier to deal with than this Austrian paperhanger.

Both Churchill and Hitler seemed to acquire this quality of presence most when they became heads of their respective governments. Hitler raved and stormed while making the rounds in the beer halls attempting to get a political party started. As First Lord of the Admiralty few people would listen to this Churchillian nonsense of a coming war. However, the context was radically different when the two became, respectively, Prime Minister and Chancellor. They not only occupied the central positions to which all faces turned, but each had a definition of what was his role to play in his moment in history.

President Kennedy is correct when he said, in effect, that the most important question is the view the executive has of the executive role itself. In this regard Churchill, Hitler, and Roosevelt were all similar in that they brought to their respective tasks a specific concept of administration. History knows of their common quality as autocratic. Although one must be careful in suggesting that these men lived autocratic lives, one certainly need not flinch at the statement that they were for the most part known in their administrative roles as autocrats, having rare and delicate mixtures of the other two styles.

For example, Churchill tended to have the bureaucrat's petty compulsiveness about him, which Stalin and Roosevelt found amusing and which Eisenhower found exasperating. Hitler was not very tidy, but he was compulsively obstinate in his administrative affairs to the point that his chiefs of staff could not move him from his set position. He might overwhelm them with his vigorous presence, but he was usually immune to the personal advances of his chief advisors.

The ambiguity in understanding the executive role is found in the need to use all three units of administration. The executive who leans strongly toward the autocratic style relies upon himself, the bureaucrat upon his system, and the democrat upon his group. But all three, that is, individual, system, and group, are interwoven in any activity. In the home, for example, there are separate individuals, each capable of thinking and acting completely independently of the other members of the family. But the family may also act as a group in which these separate individuals are emotionally united. Of course, there are orderly ways to maintain separate identities and to unite in common endeavor. These rules and regulations are as much instruments of the individual as of the group. They arise through the organized activities of the family and generally the actions and thoughts of the group are similar to those of the individual members.

A clean distinction between autocratic and bureaucratic is difficult also because both are power systems that overlap considerably. Theoretically, one is to acquire the power of authority and the other the power of order. In many cases actions that are described as autocratic may also be somewhat bureaucratic. For example, the autocrat follows the formula of giving to his subordinates the minor or detail jobs, reserving for himself the major or crucial ones. This inevitably makes for a bureaucratic system of petty details being chased by ambitious subordinates. The autocrat is more favorably disposed to the bureaucrat than the latter is to the former. Far more distinct, however, are these two from the democratic type. Some executives may come to the mind of the reader as perfect examples of the autocrat. It must be cautioned, however, that inwardly they may be more or less autocratic than their behavior seems to suggest.

The Power Ethic

The effective autocrat seldom uses more than a few of the ingredients presented in this discussion. He uses those that will assure successful implementation and maintenance of his power drive. This power mix will vary with each personality.

Power is his basic mechanism for getting on in the world

and he generally has a rather strong impulse to rationalize power in terms of social utility and moral necessity (this is not true of the neurocrat; see Chapter 8). For the autocrat power is to the social world what gravity is to the physical world. It is a social necessity, the stuff from which the bureaucrat's love for order is derived. Without the exercise of power, organization could be neither established nor maintained. Within an organization use of power guards against anarchy. Its use is the autocrat's most important responsibility and one he cannot wield indifferently.

Furthermore, the autocrat senses that power is the source of success and the cause of failure, and must therefore be treated with diligence and respect. The autocrat does not necessarily have a mystical awareness of the magic of power, but he is likely to have an almost naïve faith in it. It is an emotional crutch that helps him hobble when otherwise he would fall helpless (see the discussion of the neurocrat, Chapter 8).

In order to meet the reality needs of his administrative responsibility, the executive must objectify the power impulse, that is, use it to serve the realistic needs of his organization. If power is used to attain realistic goals, the further acquisition of power becomes an executive function or skill. Although the acquisition of power may be legitimate in itself, power may still corrupt the person who strives to gain it, and this possible evil is to be guarded against.

Autocratic power has an arbitrary aspect to it. It is found in the executive's capacity to modify others' behavior as he desires and at the same time resist modifying his own behavior in a manner he does not desire. This is accomplished with delicate skill. Counseling with autocratic executives suggests a keen awareness of the difference between power and authority. Authority is seen as the recognized right to use power, but it is not power itself. An executive may have power over others without authority to use it. He may also lack power to use the authority he has.

Much autocratic power is derived from superior knowledge, ability to decide and command, or magnetic personality. Consider the president of one large corporation. His resonant voice and contagious exuberance command immediate attention. Wherever he goes he dominates his environment. This man was initially given the organizational authority which he now holds because he had acquired a wide sphere of personal power. Because his ability to control others far exceeds that normally attributed to his position, his power exceeds his authority. Consider, on the other hand, the executive who gives an order that is not carried out. His power is less than his authority. His subordinate, by disobedience, is increasing his own power at the expense of his superior.

The autocrat aspires to power greater than his authority. The bureaucrat, of course, does not. Self-rule is the autocrat's need. Unlike the bureaucrat he is seldom concerned whether his power is based on authority. This is the secret of his success, but also sometimes the basis of his failure. He may make the mistake of extending his power so far beyond his authority that he becomes vulnerable.

For this reason, the autocrat may direct his efforts to accomplish two things. The first is to persuade authority-granting groups, such as boards of directors, to give him additional authority to back up the power he has already acquired. The second is to eliminate any elements that power skills cannot control.

Notice, he attempts always to advance his power beyond his authority and later to get authority to support his power. Force is seldom used because it is not always effective. Force is translating executive power into the most extreme form of action and it may demonstrate waning power or the abuse of power. The executive who fires a subordinate who did not carry out an order is employing force, but the action succeeds because of authority.

The true essence of autocratic power is predictability. The executive whose orders are obeyed has power. If, over a period of time, they are always obeyed, the consequences of any future command can be reliably predicted. When force must be used, the results are not reliably predictable. The replacement for the man fired may be unable to carry out the order, performance may be delayed, other men may quit in sympathy. That is why force seldom increases power, but draws upon power without replenishment. Except for the bully type, the autocrat is always careful in his use of force.

Above all, he does not base his drive for power on status, for status is not power. Status refers to the relative position, rank, or standing that an individual has in the organization. One who stands high in the hierarchy might not have as much power as another with lower rank. The autocrat may use status symbols to show that he is important and powerful. However, the power that appears to come with status is actually a characteristic of the position. Status may symbolize power, but it cannot substitute for it.

Popularity is not power. An executive may be powerful, but not generally popular. Genuine executive conflict is rarely settled by a popularity vote, but usually resolved by differences in power. At least this is what the autocrat typically believes. He may be so convinced that power and popularity are unrelated that he may make no attempt to become popular. In fact, he is quite proud at times that he is not the most liked figure in the organization. He often preaches that one need not have to run a popularity contest to be a good executive. He does not cultivate the garden personality.

In short, authority, status, and popularity have little meaning for the executive without the immediate support of power and the ultimate sanction of force. And whatever authority, status, and prestige the autocrat has can be preserved by his ability to control others who are capable of granting and withholding these important attributes. Hence, his drive for self-rule.

Power Exercises

The power drive of the autocrat is often well received. The fact of the matter is that executive power has been generally and most conveniently acquired by unremitting pursuit of it. To be sure, this pursuit must be honorable and orderly and must recognize the needs and goals of the organization. Nevertheless, only rarely does business give power to the executive who does not seek it; nor is it given to the executive who seeks it for his own ends. The ideal in many organizations is to give power to those who both want it and will use it for the ends of the organization. The idea seems to be that the individual who does not actively seek power is not typically accustomed to its use and effects. There is little proof that the self-sacrificing individual is more capable of dealing with power than one who actively seeks it.

It is customary in business for the autocrat to seek more power just as it is for him to wield effectively the power he already has. Power is dynamic and volatile. Because it can change masters at any moment, power is not easily subject to monopolistic control. Only those who make a practice of understanding power can really get enough to do anything worthwhile. This is made clearer by the fact that in the business organization every job has a sphere of influence and consequently every job has an effect on the performance of some other job.

In a sense, the holder of a job represents the power of the organization focused in one individual. This positional power tends toward permanence because the power structure of the organization tends to become fairly fixed over a period of time. This means that positional power is highly predictable. The occupant, no matter who he is, must fulfill certain basic duties and responsibilities.

However, unlike the bureaucrat, the autocrat is not a robot who mechanically transmits the power the organization gives him through his position. It takes skill to operate effectively as an agent of power for the organization. This brings into play his personal power skills which enable him to translate positional power into effective action. Besides using his personal skills to fulfill the obligations of his particular position, he may use them to go beyond his authorized power.

The autocrat is typically not content with whatever power goes with his office. In fact, we think of a powerful executive as a man whose influence is not circumscribed by a manual of job responsibilities. He creates the greater share of his power by applying his inner resources. In short, the autocrat not only attempts to transmit power, but also generates it.

If much ability is required to exercise the power that comes with a position, even greater ability is required to extend one's power over vast stretches of activity with comparative ease and effectiveness. This is made more difficult by the fact that organizations understandably resist extension of power beyond prescribed limits. If they did not, autocrats would quickly build up a number of power camps, each seeking to overcome the others. Rather than risk crumbling, organizations prefer rigidity, even at the danger of slow death through structural stagnation. However, the genius of modern organization is that it has built-in rewards that challenge executives to incur the risk that comes with the drive toward expansion. A major reward is power itself.

Even if there were no organizational prohibitions against expansion of executive power, there still would be grave risk in the tendency to guard one's already acquired power. Both the autocrat and the bureaucrat tend to believe there is only so much power to be divided in any organization. If one individual acquires more power, he must take it from someone else. Actually, the executive may get a bigger slice of the power pie by increasing the total size of the pie, but this fact is not easily demonstrated.

The bureaucrat has found a way to escape this tension-ridden situation. Rather than try to extend his personal power against the resistance of others, he tries to gain power by being promoted to a higher position. But to go up he believes that he must do exactly what his position calls for and not attempt to gain influence beyond this accepted orbit. Consequently, he appears unambitious, loyal, expert, and unegotistical. He is, in short, a man of the system. Naturally, he wants everyone else to play the game his way or the structure might change and thereby reduce his chances for promotion. The autocrat views this kind of an executive as a weakling who cannot attempt to mount the organizational ladder by the pursuit of power because inwardly he is not capable of undergoing the intense struggle.

Closely related to how power is acquired is how it is exercised. This raises the question of what executive power skills are. Power is maintained and increased through exercise. Each form of power activity becomes more perfect by practice. Naturally, higher uses are more concerned with refined power skills. We often think of power in terms of an executive who throws his weight around. This kind of exercise is common. Power under any name spells domination. But what distinguishes the lower uses from the higher exercises is the degree to which power is disguised.

The mature autocrat considers the most refined power skill the ability to control others without letting them know it. To make others act as he wants is power; to make them want to act his way is supreme power. If the truth were known, we would be surprised how much we act according to the aims and wishes of others. We should not be upset, however, for the fact that so much of what we do is done willingly attests to the success of power and not to its abuse.

What separates the men from the boys is the ability to influence others on one's own terms without appearing to be domineering. Few are able to achieve this higher skill. We shall describe autocratic skills and try to indicate whether they are higher or lower power exercises.

Self-Help

The autocratic executive generally makes his influence felt by the things he says and does directly. If he tends to underemphasize the subtlety of power, his subordinates base their expectations on what they see of him. They watch him all the time because they need cues from him to determine their proper course of action. Whether his cues are carefully given or not, the executive will rely heavily on their being received as intended.

By this means he develops a common understanding that his subordinates are to receive stimuli and he is to send them out. The matter of exchange is dependent upon the need he has for information and aid from them. Generally, when informing and advising him, the subordinate does not know how much the executive already knows. He is to be told everything and they are to be told only what is required for maximum performance.

The very act of administering establishes a gulf between the superior and subordinate. It is a gulf which the superior may freely bridge, but which may not be bridged by return action on the subordinate's part, except by his request. In practice this means that whatever power is transmitted from the superior to the subordinate is transmitted as a temporary condition for achieving explicit commands. It is not formalized into set positions. This would constitute too much sharing of authority and power without the necessary controls. The cumulative effect is monopolization or centralization of power. This is the practical meaning of autocracy or one-man rule.

The autocrat will dominate to the point of triviality. Stalin was an absolute autocrat to the point of lunacy. His practice of detail immersion prohibited others from taking action if he did not. Nobody could make an independent decision. Even taking leave of his presence had to be preceded by a command of dismissal. Everyone became completely dependent upon this autocrat who used them as he saw fit. Nothing was too big or too little for Napoleon's attention. In a letter he wrote only two days before the battle of Moscow, he gave instructions on how wide the streets should be made in Vichy. One would think that the autocrat could allow subordinates to act independently on such a matter—but not Napoleon, however, nor most autocrats.

Autocrats are often criticized because they cannot relinquish trivial control points. Sewell Avery, former board chairman of

Montgomery Ward, had over fifty top executives come and go in the 1940s alone because none was allowed to act independently. Avery was totally unable to delegate even minor authority and when he did he took it back with aggressive regret. He wanted nobody near the throne.

Executives are always told to leave details to others. To the autocrat this is a rather naïve presumption born of laziness or timidity. The autocrat needs to know what is going on. He disagrees with the democrat's concept of getting information through counsel from others. There is no substitute for immersing oneself thoroughly in what is going on. Besides, he must know how to judge the information supplied by others. He must have a frame of reference. Exposure to details of operations and policy is necessary to know what information is needed. In addition, he knows that subordinates often do not tell him everything or often tell him only what he wants to know. To avoid this, he may have a separate intelligence system which exists independently of his line subordinates. He helps himself to everything he needs to get the job done. He reaches far down into the ranks without concern for the domain of authority that he might violate. He practices self-help.

The big problem is not to lose himself in details to the point that the needs and goals of the organization or powers to be are lost. General du Pont found great relaxation in detail immersion to the point that detachment from the details left him dissatisfied and ineffective. He was able to expand his competency across vast stretches of trivia and at the same time give a sensitive and responsible reputation to the firm. But this ability to keep both perspectives is rare and usually causes severe crisis. The successor, for example, to the General was incapable of such competency with trivia.

Detail immersion is the father of crisis management. Crisis

management has a distinct role in administrative history. It is a product of detail immersion and the autocrat's tendency to control through creating crises. The latter is a product of his desire to keeps things in a state of flux and never allow complacency to reign. He controls by overwhelming. The panic button provides his administrative identity.

When a crisis does descend upon an organization for whatever reason, the autocrat is quick to make the most of it. He is then in his element. If he is effective at all, he is effective at this time because in a crisis his arbitrariness may receive least resistance. Consequently, a crisis brought on by detail immersion is effectively resolved by the autocrat's other characteristic of responding quickly and dispassionately. The two characteristics of decisiveness and triviality are offsetting. They may together be called detail decisiveness.

Both autocrats and democrats may practice detail immersion. However, detail snooping is not usually authoritatively backed when done by a democrat. He usually does it to keep himself informed about the progress and needs of his subordinates. It is always a temporary pattern, for it may be regarded as an invasion of the subordinate's private domain.

The autocrat cannot "invade" anyone's private domain because no one really feels that he has any privacy nor any right to privacy. Furthermore, no one really feels involved in determining his own authority and responsibility. The autocrat attempts to minimize aggressive hostility toward him by not allowing the subordinate to feel involved enough to acquire a "proprietary" interest in what he is doing.

Because the democrat does help people to feel involved in their work and authority, he can easily invoke feelings of hostility by checking up on them. If he does detail snoop, it must always be with complete permission and acceptance of the subordinates and in service of their mutual interests.

The autocrat is just as likely to fire an individual found errant in a trifling capacity as he is to fire one who has made a major mistake, because details are important to him. The difference between a detail and a nondetail is practically indistinguishable. This closeness of opposites is reinforced because details are charged with authority. When an autocrat delegates even a detail, he may feel that he is giving up a part of his authority.

In studying business executives it is fascinating to watch how they practice detail decisiveness. They will issue orders as though their authority will not be delegated, that is, lessened, if they act with dispatch and firmness. Since they separate their authority from their orders of command, they can more or less slip out the orders without loss of authority. But this release must be done quickly or their authority will go too. Likewise, when the detail orders are received from subordinates, they are received with responsibility attached to them but no authority. The autocrat feels deprived and weakened, if not helpless, when he is not busily engaged in details.

Commanding through details is amenable to the autocratic style because it is precarious and difficult to order a vast program into action arbitrarily. If the program is taken apart piece by piece, assigned, and closely supervised, there is less possibility of resentment. Hitler's greatest resistance from his general staff came when he arbitrarily fashioned vast programs such as the invasion of Poland. His least resistance came when he arbitrarily sponsored minor events, each of which was assigned to one individual.

Not all autocrats practice detail immersion consistently.

Andrew Carnegie had a most unpredictable rhythm. One day he would be in his castle in Scotland seemingly unconcerned about the worldly affairs of running a steel company in Pittsburgh. Shortly thereafter he would be present in a board meeting in Pittsburgh challenging his chairman Frick or his president Schwab on some incidental point such as the price of coke. Not knowing where he might next set down, this fluttering figure could keep his people on their toes. Although his technique did not represent random sampling, he always seemed to find a detail or two that could justifiably—or sometimes unjustifiably—become the sole object of his total energy.

His tyrannical executive rhythm at times produced unpredictability of humorous proportions. Schwab was Carnegie's fair-haired boy for whom he acquired a father's attachment. One day he brought "Smiling Charlie" on the carpet to account for constantly rising costs. Nearing the end he turned and said, "I am told that you are personally extravagant, also. Here you are a poor country boy and you spend every cent you make." Schwab virogously denied the charge and took up the diversionary tactic of pouring out a stream of funny stories. The hours passed and roars and roars of laughter burst forth from Carnegie. The butler finally came in and informed Schwab, "Pardon me, sir, but that cabman from the Holland House says he'd like to be paid or dismissed. He's been waiting for you since nine o'clock." Schwab had the wind drawn from his sails, but Carnegie doubled over in stitches. For Schwab this proved to be disturbing because thereafter he found Carnegie all the more unpredictable.

To be unpredictable is to achieve a control over people that is seldom achieved by a more consistent pattern of detail immersion. Because of its irregularity, the subordinate must be overconscientious in attempting to avoid being vulnerable to error or the charge of irresponsibility. These two attributes, perfection and responsibility, are at the heart of the subordinate's competency.

The detailist represents a most interesting paradox. He holds himself aloof psychologically, but he is very much present administratively. This extraordinary ability to maintain one's inaccessibility while invading the subordinate's domain of trivia is a major human feat. Yet it is often done with both relish and mastery by the autocrat.

In extreme cases of autocracy the executive makes his domination of subordinates almost total. He dominates by arbitrarily assigning orders which are themselves details. He then draws back into a relatively inaccessible shell—he is unapproachable and above it all, the supreme master. The next phase may find him storming into the subordinate's office inquiring about the details of the detail he had assigned him. Here he shows an extreme dependency reaction in front of his subordinate. Put the two phases together and one can see the executive's psychological responses to the problem of ken (see Chapter 2). He may seem to waver between independence and dependence, never achieving satisfactory resolution, but he, of course, feels he is the complete master .

Self-Protection

The autocrat argues that detail immersion allows him to know what is going on and provides a framework in which to make decisions and interpret advice if and when it is asked for. This is no doubt the administrative need. The psychological need may stem from his power orientation projected into his subordinates. He may distrust them because he himself strives to offset the restraints on power and authority that others place upon him. He must protect himself. Because he often elicits the response of silent or overt hostility, he becomes wary and suspicious of his subordinates in general, and then his own acts tend to bring responses that verify his suspicions. This basic distrust of subordinates partly accounts for the monopolization of authority to the point of detail immersion. This can be illustrated by looking to almost any autocrat today, including Nehru, Adenauer, de Gaulle, Kruschchev, Franco.

In business, distrust is almost a tradition. In the early days of capitalism, business owners believed that a man who did not have a capital investment in the firm could not be expected to work diligently and honestly for another man's gain. It was quite a discovery when a few businessmen found that under certain conditions authority could be safely delegated. But these exceptional subordinates had to be tested over long periods of time for their loyalty and honesty. It took many years of experience before the businessman could place his trust in subordinates as he does today. Proven trust and loyalty are still held to be the most important basis of delegating authority.

In politics distrust is common. Truman came to the presidency just as naïve administratively as Lincoln and soon realized that the chief difficulty in trusting subordinates was that they typically had strong tendencies to arrogate responsibility to themselves. Although he claims to have eventually succeeded in surrounding himself with associates who would not overstep the bounds of delegated authority, he was still extremely careful in this matter. To make sure that he was on top of their assumption of duty he often asked for detailed reports. From Secretary of State Byrnes he required a report on foreign affairs every twenty-four hours, and when Byrnes failed to obey, he was told to resign. Trespassing upon an executive's authority might be regarded as an act of willful disobedience, but to the autocrat it is an unpardonable sin—so highly do they respect and give deference to authority.

Cleveland and Polk's avidity for details was apparently supported by a basic distrust of subordinates. But Polk believed that conscientious execution of the responsibilities of office precluded any delegation. His concern was errors. If he entrusted the details and smaller matters to subordinates, constant errors would occur. "I prefer to supervise the whole operation of the government myself than entrust the public business to subordinates, and this makes my mistakes very great."[4]

To overcome the administrative disadvantage of this basic distrust of subordinates, the autocrat will often look to cronies of long standing, to men who share his views and biases, to men of the same background and experience. In many cases this search for a "second self" produces men as much as possible like himself. It is a rare autocrat who does not eventually find men of his own kind. For this reason autocrats are well known for having "invisible advisers"—men who can advise and assist but who have no formal authority. Jackson had his kitchen cabinet, Wilson his tennis cabinet, and Roosevelt his brain trust. Kitchen cabinets are common in business. They serve as "trouble shooters" with no clearly defined roles until trouble arises. This is an informal, though quite effective, way of "spreading the executive."

After proving their loyalty and trust, the members of business kitchen cabinets often gravitate toward more permanent assignments, as in the case of Couzens and Sorenson who became Ford's finance and production chiefs. However, in more permanent positions they have formal authority which often brings out the autocrat's feelings of suspicion. Consequently,

4 Allan Nevins, *Polk*, Longmans, Green, 1952, pp. 360–361.

he ties them tightly into these jobs in ways that circumscribe their opportunity to violate his distrust. They lose their informal relation to the boss, and may find themselves being checked on by a new kitchen cabinet of eager men who are personally loyal and close to the executive. They now must be able to exist between the jaws of a vise, between the zealous member of the new kitchen cabinet and the autocrat himself. Often they will become subservient to the kitchen cabinet as well as to the autocrat. Thus, kitchen cabinets are powerful devices in the hands of autocrats.

The distrust of subordinates may become so strong that a "usurpation complex" becomes manifest. The symptom of this complex is a consistently strong reaction to subordinates who become too useful or gain too much prestige. Carnegie attempted to oust Frick, who actually made the Carnegie Steel Corporation an integrated enterprise, because he had acquired too much prestige and had begun to behave as though he owned the firm. Frick claimed that he was merely watching out for Mr. Carnegie's better interest, but Carnegie attempted, although unsuccessfully, to dislodge the chairman of his board of directors.

Subordinates can arouse the autocrat's usurpation complex by knowing too much, working too hard, gaining too many special privileges, or demonstrating too much intimacy with higher-ups. His means of self-protection is usually a large turnover of subordinates. The complex frequently becomes more intense as the executive grows older, for then the desire for power increases while the ability to maintain it wanes. Sewell Avery of Montgomery Ward seemed to show this complex increasingly as he entered his seventies. During this period he lost executives by the dozen.

Of course, there may be grounds for the autocrat's suspicions. But what appears to be an invasion of authority may actually serve an important function, the "rescue function." Stalin ruled with a ruthless inefficiency, but the system held together and worked because there were always some individuals who did what had to be done even though they were not authorized to do so. He often did not know these silent usurpers, who rescued him from his self-rule. When he did find out, he stupidly made sure that they would not violate his authority again. The rescue function occurs more frequently than the autocrat knows. When he finds out he should at least be quiet and grateful. However, if he suffers from the usurpation complex, he may misinterpret to the detriment of himself and his subordinates.

A contained distrust of subordinates allows the autocrat to keep them on their toes and to prevent complacency and contrived hostility. He pushes and drives with the aim of getting things done. Busy people both stay out of trouble and get things done.

Self-Consultation

The autocrat believes in the prime importance of individual responsibility. The concrete unit of existence is the individual and the human scene consists of interdependent individual actions based on domination and obedience. An assumption of human inequality is implied in this belief. Those who dominate do so because of superior ability, foresight, and adaptability. They arrive at superior positions of control not only because they are capable of assuming the responsibility which lesser men are not, but because they can make decisions of their own to which others must bow. Thus the autocrat places high priority on independent decision-making. To think and act alone breeds boundless independence. Independence of judgment is a singular manifestation of the autocrat's way of dealing with the executive duality.

President Jackson treated his cabinet members strictly as subordinates who were to carry out plans they were not asked to help determine. Largely indifferent to any influence other than his own perceptions of the people's welfare, he felt his judgment should be supreme. He treated his cabinet members as clerks.

Franklin Roosevelt felt that in a good organization the executive determines policy and subordinates carry it out. Most people acting for Roosevelt served as messenger boys, for he made his own decisions. Roosevelt carried off his omnipresence in rare style by making his subordinates feel that they had no right to make independent judgments. He was able to make people feel that unless he was independent of them, they could not be dependent upon him. Said Rexford Tugwell (one of Roosevelt's policy confidants), "Nothing could be done at all unless we hang together under a leader."[5]

In creative self-consultation the executive may be given advice, but his decisions are not the direct result of consultation with others. This process should be distinguished from "choice" decision-making in which several possible solutions are boiled down in consultation with others to two acceptable solutions, between which the executive must choose. Choosing between alternatives in this manner conforms to the autocratic style to the degree that the executive does not feel committed to either of the solutions presented and feels free to override either with his own solution, representing an entirely different base or an amalgam of those presented originally.

Eisenhower did not fit the autocratic style because he gen-

    [5] Arthur M. Schlesinger, Jr., *The Coming of the New Deal*, Houghton Mifflin, 1959, p. 550.

erally expected his staff to present him with a decision. This is entirely different from the currently accepted autocratic style of hearing the debaters cross-examine one another, questioning them himself and then making the decision himself. The Eisenhower staff was responsible for making the decision, although it was not responsible for the results of that decision. The autocrat's staff is a collection of individuals who inform and make suggestions to him, but they are kept at a distance to allow maximum opportunity for self-consultation. This procedure is entirely in keeping with the autocrat's belief that decisions can be made only by individuals and that when this dictum is ignored, adequate and responsible results will not be detained (see Chapter 7 for a discussion of the opposite approach).

Self-consultation is always less real than apparent. The specific act of launching a decision is naturally the act of one man. This allows the autocrat to impress others that in the act of launching there is proof of the fact of self-consultation. Those who are willing to have decisions made for them may not be aware of the extent to which self-consultation may reflect ideas acquired from others. General Henry du Pont, who for forty years autocratically controlled his firm, gleaned from departmental meetings informative ideas which now and then became translated into thunderous commands bearing his imprint of originality. Hitler's pronouncements were received as the will of the Fuehrer. Yet on several occasions he adopted gross ideas from resources other than himself. Ribbentrop, described by William L. Shirer as a man of monumental denseness, kept up a running supply of remarks and suggestions to which Hitler at times became unconsciously amenable and sometimes subservient.[6]

[6] See William S. Shirer, *The Rise and Fall of the Third Reich*, Simon and Schuster, 1960, p. 436.

Independence of judgment is more apparent than real because no human being can make decisions based solely on internal resources. The fact is that the individual is not separated from his environment. The executive operates in the midst of actions and ideas to which he cannot help but be sensitive. Complete originality may not be possible theoretically, but the autocrat must presume and show originality if for no other reason than that, to a large extent, his control is based on issuing unanticipated orders.

Although Eisenhower made extensive use of staff consultation, on a few occasions he did give high priority to his own conclusions. On one particular occasion he mastered self-consultation in grand style. During the preparation for the invasion of Europe Air Chief Marshal Leigh-Mallory protested the possible "futile slaughter" of several divisions because of the anticipated combination of unsuitable landing grounds and ground resistance. If this technical expert was correct, the crucial attack on Utah beach appeared hopeless. This meant that the whole operation "suddenly acquired a degree of risk, even foolhardiness, that presaged a gigantic failure, possible allied defeat in Europe." Eisenhower reviewed each step thoroughly and exhaustingly. "I realized, of course, that if I deliberately disregarded the advice of my technical expert in the subject, and his prediction should prove accurate, then I would carry to my grave the unbearable burden of a concience justly accusing me of the stupid blind sacrifice of thousands of the flower of our youth."[7] After much self-consultation, Eisenhower ordered that the attack go as he planned and contrary to Lehigh-Mallory's advice. The attack was successful. Self-consultation was justified.

[7] Dwight D. Eisenhower, *Crusade in Europe*, Garden City, 1952, pp. 279–282.

In the life of a typical autocrat, the act of self-consultation will occur frequently enough for him to believe that he alone "won the war" or "saved the business." Throughout history self-consultation has been responsible for many beneficial events, but also for many horrendous ones. This is the problem of the autocrat. He tends not to take advice when he needs it. Self-consultation is more than mere impulse. It involves rational deliberation and consideration of all pertinent factors.

Hitler was a genius at surprise, but made some terrible tactical errors because he was incapable of arriving at rational conclusions concerning certain subjects when he deliberated by himself. At his mountain retreat, Berchtesgarden, he made some of his most impulsive decisions, for example, the Baedeker raids, the switch from military to civilian targets in the Battle of Britain. His decision-making technique was irrational and at the same time he remained impervious to advice from his high command. Inordinate reliance upon oneself is dangerous enough, but without antecedent private or group deliberation it becomes inevitably catastrophic, bringing unanticipated and irreversible consequences.

Many of Hitler's decisions represented the second thoughts of a man who did not really have a first thought or the common sense to consult with others who did have first thoughts. His impulsive desire to hold up the Russian campaign to capture Yugoslavia allowed the Russian winter to stop the ill-clad German army from capturing Moscow and perhaps prevented the winning of the Russian campaign. Many decisions, on the other hand, were long in coming, yet he could not accept consultation with others as an alternative to indecision. Some occasions of excessive indecisiveness included running for president in 1932, opening the western front, and invading

England. The delay in the invasion of England gave valuable time to the Allies.

Arriving at decisions quickly is generally considered a characteristic of the autocrat. He may seem impulsive; he may seem to ignore the process of self-consultation. The fact that he does not appear to retire to "meditate" does not mean that he has not given full consideration to all aspects of the problem. There are some individuals who seemingly engage in self-consultation effectively on their feet. Others must hold off decisions, and still others must anticipate problems that may require private deliberation.

The autocratic style may be marked by the appearance of spontaneous decisions, but a more reliable index is the minimization of advice from others to the point of bare necessity. The autocrat strives to realize in himself the competency required to make his own decisions.

Certainty and Rigidity

The democratic executive seems to thrive on ambiguity. He enjoys the full richness of developing events before completion and the grey zones between opposites. He usually takes an enlarged view of problems, evidences an amazing patience with distraction, and foregoes many attempts to be logically tidy.

The bureaucrat cannot tolerate ambiguity. His putting-in tendency makes him overly aware of objects, things, and ideas that are out of place or do not belong. They must be "put" in their proper place. Unlike the democrat who rejoices in wholes, he likes parts and pieces that make up the whole. His administrative format is characterized by vigilance toward system and order.

The autocrat also has a low tolerance for the uncertain,

doubtful, and unreliable, and therefore he attaches himself to well-tried and accepted ideas and practices. His executive style may be characterized by never putting one foot forward unless both are first on firm ground. To accommodate this fear of the ambiguous there is a marked tendency toward unqualified thinking in terms of arbitrary diagnoses and overgeneralizations. These strong assertions are made to achieve certainty when certainty is not really felt. The object of arbitrary commands and gestures may be to substitute physical strength or verbal strength for psychological ambiguity.

Given an established administrative format, reliable experiences, and a relatively stable socioeconomic environment, the autocrat can be very effective in going to the root of trouble, simplifying problems, and achieving firm solutions. In these circumstances he far surpasses the effectiveness of the democrat and his apparent spontaneity brings freshness that the bureaucrat finds disturbing and unreliable.

But in confusing, changing, and new circumstances, such as exist today, the autocrat will impose a rigid, conventional, and superficial structure upon a crisis, although he may have to stretch the design to accommodate the differences from his experience with similar events in the past. In a crisis situation his solution will boom forth with the ring of clarity and wisdom. When everyone is anxious and uncertain, the autocrat remains strong and convincing.

Harry Truman had the autocrat's gift of reducing a complex issue to absurd but convincing proportions. Adlai Stevenson, on the other hand, saw many in-between issues which were important to consider in arriving at a proper solution. But during his two presidential campaigns the people waited for concrete, simple, and convincing solutions. They did not get them because Stevenson did not think that way. The public needed the strong hand of decision; Stevenson was content with wisdom. He lost twice largely because he was too complex when his opponent was too simple. The public sometimes loves the autocrat's simplicity.

And so may business. To the democratic personality business is a nightmare with the script written by Gertrude Stein. It is a meticulous giant that lives on a diet of routine and order, seasoned lightly with crumbs of spontaneity and love. The autocrat works with the individual situation at hand, without becoming involved in side issues or in problems of human consequence. He feels little, knows more, and does a lot. He is an unabashed conservative.

The collected wisdom of his organization is accepted and used. He does not look for problems, he selects well-proven instruments of change, he conforms to traditional patterns of authority, and he does not dissipate energy over wide ranges of activity. The autocrat's bicycle psychology allows submission to tradition, the status quo, and precedent. He in turn achieves a tight discipline of subordinates below. In this lockstep motion he can find relief from uncertainty, doubt, and freedom.

Disciplined Obedience

There is a martinet to some degree in every autocrat. It would certainly be humiliating for him if, after self-consultation, he found his firm decisions poorly received. Also, to have his communion with gods rejected by ordinary mortals is a profound threat to him. To avoid this humiliation and threat much energy is invested in keeping people in line and obedient to commands.

Discipline is the most difficult element of the autocratic style to master. Failure brings accusation of being rigid, egocentric, indifferent to others, incapable of admitting a mistake, overbearing, intolerant, suspicious, and vindictive—in short, a tyrant. If, however, the executive does master the element of discipline, others will look upon him as a giant among men, a man who has achieved for himself a degree of integrity, courage, and authority for which other men can only strive. Discipline is virtuous only when it is effective. If it is not, it becomes tyranny.

At one time overt discipline was taken for granted as the heart of the executive complex. Study of the executive styles of Rockefeller, Carnegie, Ford, Hill, De Pew, and others of their era show how threat, coercion, and intimidation were frequently used even in the first instance of insubordination. The captains of industry practiced every sort of devious dealings and condoned abominable human and business relations. The public, knowing full well what went on, simply nodded and expected little else. The brutalities condoned rivaled many of those more generally regarded as characteristic of totalitarian regimes.

To Henry Ford the tyranny of business discipline was excusable because, "A great business is really too big to be human." He never believed in the "glad hand" or the "personal touch" or the "human element." To him it was "too late in the day for that sort of thing." For the "weaklings" who knuckled under he had praise. For those who cried out for human dignity he had pity. "I pity the poor fellow who is so soft and flabby that he must always have an atmosphere of good feeling around him before he can do his work . . . unless they obtain enough mental and moral hardness to lift them out of their soft reliance on 'feeling' they are failures."[8]

[8] Henry Ford (in collaboration with Samuel Crowther), *My Life and Work*, Doubleday, 1926, pp. 190–192.

The inability of the subordinate to discipline himself has always been a major reason given for the autocrat's use of strict measures to keep people in line.

In the history of modern business the autocrat has achieved disciplined obedience partly by methods originally intended for other purposes. Minute division of labor, technological displacement of craft skills, and automation of the factory system were not adopted simply because they decreased production costs. As the workers increasingly showed their rebellious tendencies toward management, these devices became exceedingly appealing, for they achieved the integrated and controlled essence of modern large-scale organization. The technological imperative did more for the autocrat to provide disciplined obedience than all his skills of personal command and threat.

The worker today is the epitome of discipline. He comes and goes day in and day out with such a high degree of reliability that his efforts are fully predictable. Considering the mass of effort daily engaged in set tasks, the number of strikes are amazingly small. And, then, for the most part they can be predicted in advance. The autocrat of the past also became fond of enforcing bureaucratic rules and regulations among his subordinate managers for the purpose of keeping them in line. Managerial personnel in many companies today still maneuver in a lock-step motion that would make King Louis XIV or Cromwell glow with pride.

However, the martinet in the executive today is not always easily noticed. In a fluid and uncertain battlefield the martinet may reveal more openly and quickly his need to eliminate permanently all forms of deviation. However, in a close-knit business organization he cannot easily snuff out dissension among the ranks, relocate poorly trained troops, select strategically his own field of operations. Yet, if he is a true martinet, he will take great pains to acquire disciplined obedience within the organization.

One failing of the martinet is that he tends to use direct force and threat of force to the exclusion of more indirect techniques of persuasion and manipulation. And these skills might help avoid the harshness of domination. He is not able to achieve a judicious mixture of coercion and persuasion. He fails to develop an administrative rhythm that maximizes control and minimizes punishment.

As domination brings hostility, autocracy may develop into tyranny. The resentment that builds up among subordinates must be discharged somehow. It may be given release by direct hostility toward the autocrat, their peers, or their own subordinates. It may be sublimated in overconscientiousness toward details and petty regulations. It may show up indirectly in mean humor and wit, idle story-telling, and jostling and secretive activities among close friends. Usually these tendencies to resist the martinet impair his ability to achieve complete harmony between what he demands and what he gets from his subordinates. He may resort to the isopathic principle of using more control to cure problems of control—hence his overcontrol, his tyranny. Keeping people in line becomes his major chore. Not only does he find minor deviations psychologically disturbing, but he cannot afford them from an administrative point of view. He has achieved a diversified but so detailed set of coordinated functionaries that deviation amounts to disaster. As a result he must restrain with the rudeness of a tyrant.

Objective Arbitrariness

The autocratic use of power may be supplemented by personal skills that overwhelm through their logic rather than their authority. One of the most important of these techniques is objective arbitrariness.

The technique of stage director Lawrence Olivier will serve as an illustration. When questioned about whether his approach made puppets out of his actors, he replied in a manner compatible with the autocratic style: "The actor must be disciplined. He must be so trained that he automatically carries out the director's orders. I expect my actors to do exactly what I tell them to do and do it quickly so I can see my own mistakes immediately if I have gone wrong."[9] Olivier believes that the director must know the play so well that he alone knows where the action should rise or fall. Such control will not allow the actor to experience the tempo and essence of the play enough to offer intelligent suggestions. The actor will therefore be totally incompetent. Thus, the autocratic effect of superiority and inferiority is achieved. The effect is fully predictable given the hierarchical orientation of the autocrat.

All possibility of counterargument must be removed. This may be done in one of two ways. The first is to command obedience, leaving the need for discipline to be enforced by the personal actions of the executive. The subordinates are not to reason why; they must merely take his word for it, even if they have better ideas themselves that might help improve the play. But this is not the most advanced theory today. In this era of rationalism and equalitarianism, the autocrat must find a better reason than himself. He must find a means to objectify his need for obedience. Now let us again look at Olivier's technique.

Since the actor is allowed to react only to the director, he alone cannot grasp a crucial point of change or improvement.

[9] Maurice Zolotow, "The Olivier Method," *The New York Times*, Jan. 22, 1962.

Consequently, no one is in a position to refute or discredit the director intelligently: "The individual may not see the logic of an action I require him to do, but he must do it, for if the director really knows the play there is a sound reason for that action." In short, the actors are to be managed and the heart of management is discipline. The director can be arbitrary because he alone is informed and aware of what is going on. The basis of achieving this type of discipline is the "monopolization of objectivity."

Objective arbitrariness achieves for the autocrat today what the personal command did for the captain of industry. It makes the autocratic style proper and efficient. Without mastery of this delicate tool, the autocrat has only a cleaver to hack away at the jungle of human entanglement and opposition.

In an administrative format, such as the Olivier method, that brings competency to one individual to the exclusion of the rest, superior knowledge becomes the justification for arbitrary action and disciplined obedience. The superior informs and gives reasons which cannot be known or appraised by the subordinate who therefore obeys. The discipline is smooth and clean and leaves fewer problems.

Silent Autocracy

The two major techniques for keeping people in line are intimidation and seduction. (The democrat uses a third, conversion, which, unlike intimidation and seduction, is not intended to weaken the subordinate.) Intimidation is threat with implied or stated penalty, and seduction is threat with implied or stated reward, but the only real difference between the two is the degree of subtlety. Although only Henry Ford had the guts to admit to the techniques he used to keep people in line, few men in his era made any effort to be subtle. Today it simply is not good company manners to be overt about discipline. Seduction is increasingly in vogue. Seduction allows the autocrat to increase the subordinate's rights, privileges, and responsibilities if he conforms to pattern. It is not at all uncommon to upgrade the prestige, office furnishings, or personnel to accommodate the need to keep subordinates in line. In a way seduction becomes subtle intimidation for those who do not conform, because they are not granted the additional pleasures that come to those who live up to the boss's expectations.

The direct threat of firing is practically obsolete, especially among top business executives. Company manners dictate that you promote only those who are team men, which literally means those who do not fall out of role or character. It is as difficult for a deviant to get to the top as it is for a camel to go through the eye of a needle.

What the crude autocrats of the past did not realize is that maximum discipline to the point of total conformity can be maintained without blowing a single cap of emotional percussion. It can all be done by the handing out of rewards and penalties in the most discrete ways. Subtlety has proved so effective that the executive will rarely lose his head or raise his voice. The velvet-gloved iron hand is becoming very common.

But this technique makes absolute control of one's emotions essential. Some autocrats lack sufficient control of their emotions to play the game of subtle seductiveness. The late Sewell Lee Avery of Montgomery Ward often created "internal combustions" to the point of mass resignation. At times whole platoons of executives would resign because of his dictatorial style. In 1955 a vice-president and general manager charged that more than fifty top-level executives had been erased from Ward's executive roster. Although he shifted men with obvious ruthlessness, he told his stockholders that it was "just plain nonsense that the operation of this firm is under the rugged and terrorizing power of a demon dictator." Mumbling that he never made hasty or angry dismissals, he precipitated another mass resignation by charging that these latent rebels were a "culmination of a conspiracy." This autocrat, fighting against the dictatorial methods of our government at war, defied a war labor board order and was bodily carried from his office by federal troops.

The practice of silent autocracy or seduction is difficult because the autocrat tends toward the ever-increasing release of the self. Productive involvement in the acquisition of power precludes refraining from the use of power. After all, power is eagerly sought as well as respected. If he does not use his power to preserve it, others will certainly not preserve it for him. Not to use such an excellent tool when it is needed is a show of weakness, makes him vulnerable, and seems stupid and alien to many autocrats.

When the autocrat does withhold the aggressive use of his authority, it is done with mixed feelings. He is never really sure he is doing right and feels he may live to regret it in some way. But he will practice restraining if the overt use of power threatens continued use and pursuit of it. This is the language the autocrat knows best. Threat to the autocrat's power will bring judicious withholding of it.

Usually a rhythm of strong aggressive thrusts followed by silent seductive jabs develops in the autocrat's behavior routine. The autocrat's tool will be general inconsistency. He will appeal to cooperation and harmony, set about at times on a "get acquainted, let's chat" routine, or even entertain some of the damaged egos. He will judiciously guard against the need to use overt power.

Balancing Skills

Seduction is a manipulation skill. It is useful in controlling people without their being fully aware of the arbitrariness involved. Autocrats are always in need of skills that achieve the results of control and discipline without the ugly, messy disadvantages.

Currently the rage of autocrats is the dynamic realignment of subordinates. In short, keep people stirred up. It cannot be used too effectively by the bureaucrat because of the flexibility needed. It may fit the democratic style to equalize task differentials by giving some a chance at better jobs while others rotate back to tasks with less prestige. But when used by autocrats realignment is strictly a device to control through subtle manipulation. Stalin brought this technique to perfection. He would balance off aggressive and ambitious subordinates to maintain an equilibrium between him and them. In this way no one person acquired too much power.

Khruschchev is not averse to using this technique either. A powerful member of the presidium, Kirichenko, was assigned to take over the Rostov provincial party leadership. As one correspondent observed, "Even if he has been sent to Rostov merely as a trouble shooter, his absence from Moscow will give other ambitious and active men a chance to take over some of the key functions he has administered." If several men, including Aristov and Suslov, were by this move given ample opportunity to asume more active interest in new directions, Kirichenko would necessarily return with diminished authority and stature, although before the move he appeared to have more key responsibility than any other presidium member.

Hitler knew how to balance individuals through strategic conflict. To prevent conspiracy against his leadership, he encourage strife among his subordinates. Goering and Goebbels' constant plotting against each other kept them from plotting against Hitler.

He also used committees and group situations to keep his ambitious subordinates under his thumb. In the early days of the Nazi party, conflict arose between the northern faction, headed by Strasser, and the southern group, headed by Hitler. In his new party program Strasser proposed joining the Marxists in the plebiscite campaign to deprive the former king and princes of their possesions. Hitler ended the conflict by calling a meeting at Bamberg in southern Germany on a day when it was difficult for the northern faction to get away from their jobs. Being greatly outnumbered by Hitler's hand-picked leaders in the south, they were forced to capitulate and abandon their program. Many times after this struggle Hitler used group situations to manipulate his subordinates toward his own personal ends.

In the history of the American presidency, we can find numerous instances of autocratic manipulation. Jefferson knew well the art of screening himself from all responsibility by calling on Congress for advice and consent. Yet with affected modesty and deference he secretly dictated every measure which Congress seriously proposed.

Franklin Roosevelt was a master at balancing. Arthur Schlesinger Jr. remarks that some agencies seemed to be staffed on the ancient Persian theory of placing men who did not trust each other side by side, their swords on the table. "Everywhere there was the need to balance the right and the left—let Cohen and Corcoran write the act establishing the Security and Exchange Commission, but let Joe Kennedy administer

it, but flank him with Jim Landis and Ferdinand Pecora. . . .
He bypassed Hull, limited his relations to Farley, kept Wallace
at arms length, and blew hot and cold on a dozen others."[10]
He manipulated often by the accordion method of alternating
between limiting and releasing. Later Khrushchev was to adopt
the accordion principle. He might gradually increase freedom
and then tighten up, as after the Hungarian revolt.

To be sure, the manipulation of subordinates contains the
possibility of increasing the administrative strength of the
subordinate members by their proper combination. But to an
autocrat it is done first of all to accommodate his demand for
loyalty and obedience. He remains the sole effective force.

But of all the manipulative devices to keep people in line,
there is one that only the wisest autocrat knows how to use
properly. It is the strong-weak-strong sequence. To keep an
individual in line the boss will place below him a stronger,
more aggressive subordinate. This pressure from below will
keep him so harried and run down that he will have no time
to get in the boss's hair. If and when he does, the boss can
exert countervailing pressures. This squeeze play is far more
effective than promoting a stronger man to sit on top of him,
a technique which is not very subtle and makes the autocrat's
intimidation obvious. The strong-weak-strong sequence, however, is like putting the individual in a pressure chamber without his knowing it until his ears are about to pop, at which
time he is released totally dissipated and perfectly docile.

Pride and the Finality Complex

Naturally the autocrat's emotional resources reinforce his
productive experiences in his attempts to resolve the executive
duality. A man who places so much emphasis on action must

10 Schlesinger, *op. cit.*, pp. 543–555.

necessarily have a strong dose of pride. The autocrat is proud of his feats of independent judgment and action.

This pride is illustrated by football commissioner Bert Bell. Baseball's Ford Frick, basketball's Maurice Podoloff, and hockey's Clarence Campbell have all recognized that tsars of sport have been obsolete since the death of the autocrat Kenesaw Mountain Landis. However, Bell operated very much in terms of his own consultations, approximating the authority of Judge Landis. He has always tried to fit the game to his needs and perspectives rather than fit himself to the game.

In the course of testifying before the House subcommittee seeking to establish whether professional sports should be subject to antitrust laws, Bell defied his team owners and suddenly recognized the players' union. Subcommittee Chairman Emanuel Celler congratulated him for the move and assumed that he took this historic move upon advice of the owners. Bell calmly replied, "I did not confer with the owners or anybody else." Few can appreciate the intense excitement and satisfaction that comes to the autocrat at this moment when he can show off his accomplishments.

President Eisenhower, whose most eminent quality is perhaps charm, found opportunity to show this deep pride during a television speech on the eve of the 1960 election. He recalled in careful detail that "event in the tent" which was probably the most pivotal decision of the Allied campaign. One could not fail to note how important that moment was to him. Rarely, if ever, did he show this pride about decisions for which he was responsible as president. Perhaps the White House was too modern, warm, and populated in contrast to a tent. Or perhaps, as many suspect, he overrelied upon staff consultation. In any case, the recall of the event in the tent was a sublime moment for him.

The habit of independent decision is an expression of the executive's art. He is moved into a state of personal creativity. Many are quick to attribute independence of judgment to a kind of sadistic desire to engulf other individuals. This may be true, especially of the autocrat. But it is not the whole truth. When one has felt the creative spark of self-consultation, he seeks opportunities to keep it alive.

Called to lead during Britain's time of crisis, Churchill was delighted with the opportunity to employ all of his genius and energy in a cause he so passionately believed in. He believed he knew what orders should be issued. He made his own decisions. "I felt as if I were walking with Destiny." President Taft, who also had a fondness for making his own decisions and was accused at times of acting like a dictator, said that it was a privilege to play the part of universal providence and "set all things right."

Dealing with problems involving thousands, or perhaps millions, of people or dollars can recall the childhood feeling of helplessness in the face of towering arbitrary parents. This feeling of helplessness can perhaps be surmounted by the act of solitary decision-making, by clinging to a concept of power such as Churchill's destiny or Taft's universal providence. The desire to view things with a sense of grandeur may become so great that decisions begin to take on the appearance of finality. The finality complex seems to be a disease of many autocrats. Near the end of his life Franklin Roosevelt seemed to believe that his pronouncements had the character of insight into the universe. After the war Field Marshal Alanbrooke described Churchill as an erratic leader who was sometimes "most brilliant" and sometimes "most dangerous," and who "never had the slightest doubt that he had inherited all the military genius of his great ancestor [The Duke of Marlborough]."

A symptom of the finality complex is the presentation of decisions as the absolute solution to all problems. The autocrat typically displays some of this finality in his gestures and commands. Through decisiveness he achieves a symbolic union with the powers that usually are attributed to great men and to gods. Startling successes, such as Hitler had early in World War II, are sometimes enough to enhance an over-evaluation of oneself. In such extreme cases, even God may take on the appearance of an ambitious subordinate with active tendencies toward usurpation.

The Paternalist

The autocrat may not find his executive repertory complete until he masters manipulation of the human psyche. When this is done he achieves total domination of his subordinates that is seldom perceived as such. For all practical purposes, they are more obedient than when this manipulation of their inner dynamics is left to chance or circumstance. A form of hero worship may result from proper manipulation.

The paternalistic autocrat bases his administrative format on many of the autocratic ingredients already discussed. He must, however, achieve a piercing sensitivity to his people's psychological needs. He meets their needs to be obedient and submissive to a decisive individual who will sacrifice in order to assume responsibility for them. The autocrat becomes a parental figure.

His relations with others are highly charged with controlled ambivalence. People tend to react with love and hate toward superior power and authority. Their experiences as children provide knowledge of the essential qualities of both restrictive and releasing power. Parents withhold and grant presumably out of love for the child. Conditional love is the agency for

the transmittal of authority. Just as the father gives and withholds his love, depending upon whether the child pleases him,
the executive gives and withholds in his relations with his
subordinates. The paternalist is an autocrat disguised as a
parent. He practices seduction with a familial touch.

He practices a variation on objective arbitrariness. His control is based on irrational feelings in the human psyche rather
than on mere logic and knowledge. If the paternalist appears
arbitrary it is because in his infinite wisdom he knows best
what his subordinates need or want. It is out of love for them
that he disciplines or is rude to them. When he is not disciplining he is surprising his subordinates with benefits. Whether he
is disciplining or benevolent, he is always loving. He can do no
wrong and can control with infinite certitude and charm. His
technique, of course, is to reinforce the feelings of respect
accorded parental figures and to repress the hostile feelings.

As a seducer he may be either parent. As mother he performs the role of loving. He gives freely of his time, energy,
and money, or that of the organization or some other individual. He cannot stand to see his subordinates suffer and fears
for their safety. He cautions about taking care on trips for the
company and on vacations with the family. He is simply won-
derful.

As a father he plays the role of showing his subordinates
what is proper and correct, efficient and desirable. He advises
and counsels about the more masculine expectations he has of
them, their use of language, style of conduct, and matters of
activities. He must, of course, in this role discipline and withhold privileges. He must break up sibling rivalry and quell
disobedience.

Above all, he must protect the organization much as the
father protects the family. To this end he inspires his sub-

ordinates to work hard, keeping in mind the enemies without who are always trying to deprive the organization of the fruits of its labor. This means hostility must be showed toward outside groups, especially competitors. If not hostility, then superiority. Genuine examples of superior achievement among them must be highly praised. Consequently, the organization becomes a tightly knit family with morale and productivity the symbols of success. But, of course, no one has an effective voice because the autocrat who intermittently plays father and mother monopolizes the necessary life-giving and life-sustaining forces for their survival.

Few can play the paternalistic role well. Most autocrats move in and out of the irrational zones of the human psyche but never really capitalize upon their excursions. Trujillo, former dictator of the Dominican Republic, was a rarity. For thirty years he maintained his absolute control through remarkable will power, cunning, and ruthlessness, overcoming all obstacles in the way. He was called "Benefactor" because he had brought the nation from chaos and bankruptcy to its position as the affluent Caribbean showcase of the Latin Americas. He established minimum wages, enacted labor legislation, and improved living conditions to a level extremely high by Central American standards. Building roads, schools, hospitals, and successfully fighting disease, hunger, and illiteracy no doubt accounted for the considerable gratitude continuously being bestowed upon the "Benefactor."

But there were grave signs that his paternalism was reaching the point of diminishing returns. Increasing resistance from within and without, a drastic slowdown in the economy, matched by increasing oppressive rules and restrictions diminished his benefactor halo. Finally, his desperate show of force and unrestrained passion upset the balanced forces of love and hate. Shortly after his assassination, the full weight of the peoples' hate, long repressed by his familial touch, reduced the fallen dictator's image to ashes.

The Power Vacuum

There are many disadvantages to the autocratic style. (They are discussed also in the chapters dealing with bureaucrat and democrat.) Probably the most crucial disadvantage is the autocrat's tendency to leave a power vacuum.

The autocrat's view of his role precludes developing strong, capable replacements. Since his subordinates are kept in line and given only very limited responsibility, they learn almost nothing about the administrative intricacies which one of them will perhaps some day inherit. Or they become so submissive to authority that they lose the ability to act and decide on their own.

When one of them finally succeeds the autocrat, he may fail to respond as aggressively as his predecessor's administrative format demands. If he does not have firm control, small details and small people may prove unmanageable. Under such conditions a power struggle will develop such as when Stalin died. Malenkov proved unable to perform within the format laid down by Stalin or to change it and control the changes others were making. A power struggle ensued until resolution by Khrushchev.

It requires a great deal of flexibility to avoid leaving a power vacuum. Usually autocrats treat their subordinates equally. This is the democratic element in autocracy—all are equally inferior before the boss. To avoid a power vacuum an autocrat may designate a replacement in advance of his leaving. But designating is not enough, for the replacement may not be able to survive the power struggle that will inevitably follow. The autocrat must actually train him for the job.

But the autocrat's system of equality is broken when he begins to train any one individual. Furthermore, that one individual is placed in trying circumstances. He begins to be feared and distrusted by his colleagues and, if not sufficiently trusted by his boss, the strain may be too much for him. Consequently, actual authority must be given him. He must be moved up above other subordinates and assume responsibility for them. Only then will a power vacuum be avoided, and even this is not always a sure-fire remedy.

In any case, the autocrat must delegate much authority, which, of course, is difficult for him to do. Some autocrats feel so disturbed at the possibility of being succeeded that they change their minds and succeed themselves. But once an autocrat makes a definite move out, a power struggle develops. If he then decides to change his mind and stay, he must resolve the emerging struggle, which could prove difficult.

For example, when Adenauer saw that he could not determine his successor in his own way, he took up the notion that he could make the German figurehead presidency into a position of power and maintain his leadership from that position. But a bitter struggle developed with Erhard. Had Adenauer adequately trained a successor, he could have avoided this costly struggle. But as is true of most autocrats, he could not train a successor. Postwar West Germany regarded him with veneration for ten years and admired the high-handed methods that earned him the sobriquet of "democratur," a word coined from "democrat" and "dictator." But the struggle to fill the power vacuum brought into question for the first time the judgment of the "democratur." His monopoly of authority has been made much more difficult, if not tenuous.

De Gaulle has also created the problem of succession. In fact, one of France's most serious long-range problems is how to keep Gaullism after De Gaulle has gone. The Fifth Republic is specifically tailored to his measurements, as would be expected in the case of an autocrat. De Gaulle was recently approached about the problem and allowed a memorandum to be drawn up which presented two weaknesses of the autocratic style in general. "It described these as one man government in which De Gaulle is surrounded by monsters who lack real influence or national prestige; and the lack of any orderly system of succession."[11] But to an autocrat, these are basically bureaucratic problems needing bureaucratic attention. De Gaulle promptly assigned a core of staff to think about them.

Executives who basically distrust subordinates cannot easily begin a program for an orderly plan of succession. Autocrats immersed in the grandeur of total authority are not prone to think of stepping down. When they do step down, it is with the feeling of temporary adjustment until they can pick up the baton again. Or it is with such a sense of finality that, like George Eastman, founder of Kodak, departure from the company requires departure from this earth. At 78, old and ill but firm in purpose, he lay down in his bedroom with a folded towel on his chest and calmly ended his life with a pistol shot. A note to his friends read simply, "My work is done. Why wait?" He was followed after his death by a team of administrators, none of whom was strong enough to dominate the others.

In conclusion, the autocratic executive must be masterful and singularly competent. He is the key to all activity going on about him. Things cannot be done without him. His

[11] C. L. Sulzberger, "Foreign Affairs," *The New York Times*, July 2, 1960.

superiors or authority-granting groups and subordinates over-rely upon him in their different ways. Neither group may move against him without obviating his competency or provoking his consternation. The autocrat uses his subordinates, invades their domains of triviality, keeps them at a distance, makes his own choices and decisions, practices intimidation and seduction. He attempts to control people below on behalf of the wishes and needs of people above. The ultimate is to so control some in the interest of others that he becomes the one to whom all must turn. He becomes the sole effective force. He is an autocrat.

CHAPTER 6

THE BUREAUCRAT

The autocrat attempts to dominate the responsibilities that bombard the executive. While he serves higher authority to achieve respect, support, and power, he controls subordinates by keeping them dependent upon him. The autocratic formula is predicated upon aggressive action directed by the hierarchical orientation.

A different executive style is to direct aggressive action by the systematic orientation. The bureaucratic response is an attempt to deal with the executive responsibilities by a rationally devised set of procedures and functions integrated about an over-all policy or goal. By frequent use these rules and regulations develop into a system to which superiors and subordinates alike give deference. The problems of how, when, and whom to serve and control are largely resolved by consulting the system. Relations to superiors and subordinates are predicated upon the needs and functions of the system. Human relationships achieve a high degree of formality and uniformity.

Both autocracy and bureaucracy are at base power styles. In fact, bureaucracy is a special variation of autocracy and may precede or follow or even be concurrent with autocracy. Autocracy is one-man rule, bureaucracy is rule by rules. The one aims at making things happen, the other at making things orderly. The man of action becomes the man of logic. Productivity is replaced by efficiency. The system rather than the executive becomes indispensable. Bureaucracy is subtle autocracy.

The Emergence of the Bureaucrat

The bureaucrat is as old as human organization. He existed in early Egypt, in imperial Rome and China, and in the national monarchies of Europe. However, in the seventeenth and eighteenth centuries national legislations showed growing strength as a means of government. In modern states complex individual growth emphasized the need for economic and social legislation which called for a vast growth of administrative functions of government. The bureaucrat began to emerge in full regalia when permanent and nonelective officials secured power to apply and even to initiate means of control over the national administration and economy.

The bureaucrat became still more important as people turned to government for help and defense. Max Weber pointed out that in a centrally planned society, bureaucratic tendencies would mount with a flurry. The division of labor needed to accommodate the increased governmental services and the use of special skills in administration would increase to a point where a "dictatorship of the bureaucrats," rather than a "dictatorship of the proletariat," would result.[1]

Weber felt that a bureaucratic dictatorship would constitute a despotism unparalleled even by the ancient Egyptian

---

[1] See Max Weber, *The Theory of Social and Economic Organization,* Oxford University Press, 1947.

tyrants. It would be more oppressive because it would be efficiently oppressive. He saw and dreaded the growth of the bureaucratic mind. It is as if "we were deliberately to become men who need 'order' and nothing but order, who become nervous and cowardly if for one moment the order wavers, and helpless and torn away from their total incorporation in it." Weber saw the horrible demise of human affairs if one day the world was filled with nothing "but those little cogs, little men clinging to little jobs and striving towards bigger ones."

As the bureaucrat grew in number and importance in government, he also grew in related institutions. Business and industry were developing into amorphous masses of human protoplasm that seemingly lacked integrating vitality and manageable proportions at the top. The autocrat never delegated authority or formed practical hierarchical relationships that incorporated administrative experts and never formalized regulatory controls over them. These autocrats were great entrepreneurs but were unable to give permanence and continuity to the results of their genius.

That era may be illustrated by the founder of General Motors, William C. Durant, who integrated a large number of firms by his genius-like promotional ability. Like so many of his autocratic predecessors, including Commodore Vanderbilt, who boasted that he carried his office in his hat, Durant was a walking dictionary of vital facts and statistics interpreted by an intuitive approach to decision-making. His one-man method of making decisions was implemented by yes-men whose right to existence was justified by total loyalty and obedience. Personal inspiration accounted for his gathering around him effective subordinates who played their roles loyally. Often, however, they helped rescue their boss from errors of his self-rule.

Durant had many of the difficulties of the typical autocrat.

He could not take advice or recognize the need for order and system, especially for such important administrative functions as accounting and inventory control. He could change direction and policies just as often as he could open and close doors to his subordinates' offices. At the same fast rate big men came and went with his executive flurries.

Finally, near bankruptcy called for the development of a new systematic approach to the administrative responsibility. Du Pont performed a "lifesaving" operation and installed Alfred Sloan's plan to reorganize a new General Motors administrative format. This style was based upon the systematization of managerial authority and responsibility and the introduction of bureaucratic skills. At the same time, other administrative characteristics were adopted which later became known as the democratic view. Sloan set up the organizational mechanism of formal committees and informed discussions to resolve major issues.[2]

By the late 1930s, the reorganization of American business and industry was well on its way. The bureaucratic manager with his set of orderly, precise administrative skills gradually replaced the heroic adventuresome autocrat. This rebellion against impulsiveness reached a high point in a movement which developed with the emergence of the bureaucratic type of executive. This movement, known as scientific management, was resisted by the autocrat as neither scientific nor management.

Several observers around the turn of the century noted that division of labor or specialization was developing largely by the "drifting process." That is, the efforts of labor were ordered and reordered into different channels and forms by impulsive, erratic decisions emanating from autocratic adminis-

[2] See Ernest Dale, *The Great Organizers*, McGraw-Hill, 1960.

trations. These observers, including Frederick W. Taylor, Louis D. Brandeis, Henry Gantt, Frank B. Gilbreth, and Harrington Emerson, set out to war against inefficiency under the banner of the "one best way."

Their first principle was the systematic use of experience, the careful analysis of projects with reference to existing records and previous standards of performance. New undertakings were to be revised in the light of past experiences and directed toward clearly defined ideals of efficiency. This represented the most satisfactory way to obtain predictable results.

Thus scientific management was based on conserving the best of the past, organizing the present around an ideal of efficiency, and forecasting and planning for the future. In order to systematize and organize all existing desirable conditions, careful objective surveys were to be made to record all activities. Everything was to be standardized and all standards noted in the survey. All information would then be arranged, classified, and filed. Order became the effective instrument of administration. "A place for everything and everything in its place," was applied to personnel as "A place for everyone and everyone in his place." In short, "The right man in the right place," each performing the "one best way."

These scientific managers were attempting to reduce impulsiveness and spontaneity. One of them, Harrington Emerson, placed the objective clearly before the emerging profession. After noting that in the earlier days of manufacturing the entrepreneur often knew what he intended to make and how to make it, in large plants he noted that workers and their foremen at the lower end of the line organization were so far from "the 'little Father' or from the 'Big Stick' who dictates all policies, who alone is responsible for the organization, for delegation of power, and for supervision, that they are driven to create minor ideals and inspirations of their own, these being often at variance with the ideals of those above them."[3] Thus the new efficiency cult was aimed directly at the foundation of autocracy. By yielding to the objectively verifiable "one best way," performed by "the right man in the right place," the personal decisiveness and impulsiveness of the autocrat were to be obviated.

However, much of the autocratic style was preserved. Unity of command, discipline, singleness of direction were spelled out in ways to conform to the requirements of efficiency. The autocrat's hierarchical orientation became formalized into the scalar chain which is represented by a string of supervisors, ranging from the ultimate authority to the lowest rank. However, respect for the line or chain of authority was to be reconciled with the need to be efficient and orderly.

The impact of this cult of efficiency naturally brought increasing routinization of skill and performance. Since skill was the worker's primary basis of achieving security and usefulness, the efficiency cult helped to make him feel insecure. A rebellion ensued and brought on monumental governmental regulations and powerful unions, which in turn caused production costs to rise sharply so that further mechanization and later automation became economically feasible and necessary.

Automation is merely an advanced emphasis on superior productivity. It aims at completely eliminating the possibility of human intervention, except at a few key points of decision or in case of breakdown. The ideal under automation is not a productive worker. Individual productivity is not important, but rather the productivity of the system. Consequently, the ideal worker today is one who is reliable, regular, and steady

[3] Harwood F. Merrill, *Classics in Management*, American Management Association, 1960.

and capable of changing his routine as often as technological innovation requires. Unless the worker can put himself into a systematic work habit, devoid of any creative quality, he will not do well.

To ensure that the putting-in tendency (see pp. 91–97) will operate favorably, workers are in turn given elaborate working conditions, security, and pay of the most impersonal kind. Wages are not based upon performance because meaningful performance in terms of skill and creative satisfaction is not incorporated into work, but rather wages are based on the relative power of unions who represent the worker's need for security and recognition.

Unfortunately, such a widespread tendency to reduce all actions to systematic routine and habit could not be contained on the one level of factory work. It gradually moved into office administration and up into middle management. The safe, sure, reliable, steady mentality emerged finally at the top to battle it out directly with the impulsiveness and daring of the autocrat.

From 1910 to 1950 administrative costs rose from 13 percent to 25 percent of production costs. In increasing numbers of companies administrative costs became greater than production costs. This increase was due largely to the greater number of people needed at middle and top levels of management in proportion to the fewer workers required to operate the increasingly automatic production processes. The bulging middle and upper levels created the problem of how to manage management. The greater need for upper managerial talent required recognizing middle management ranks as a repository for future top executive talent.

Top administrative positions are increasing at a phenomenal rate. In many companies the expense of employing administrators is greater than the operating expense. Cameron Hawley has estimated that typical American and European firms have about four times as many salaried employees as hourly wage workers. The top executive group numbers nine for a European firm and forty-two for the American. "Here in the United States we have the most expensive industrial management on earth."[4] The secretarial staff required has expanded almost four times as much as the increase in administrative staff in the last twenty years. For the year 1961, 600,000 additional secretarial employees will be needed.

To equip this most expensive management in the world with efficient and proper skills, numerous agencies and institutions have been established, including private and public consulting firms and educational organizations, the least of which is the professional business administration school.

As chief executives themselves felt the restraints of the growing bureaucracy, fears arose that the dynamic and aggressive attitude of the autocrat was being hurtled into oblivion and that, as bureaucrats replaced autocrats, the essential creativity and spontaneity of the business system would be destroyed. Panaceas were offered to control the growth of what many called the civil service mentality. Probably the most widespread panacea, decentralization of authority and decision-making, was aimed directly at restoring executive initiative in the face of growing bureaucratic rigidity. The results were paradoxical. The more top management tried to decentralize decision-making, the more it had to centralize it. Experience showed that, although some degree of initiative had been restored, decentralization required so many countercontrols, rules, and procedures in the forms of reports, communications,

---

[4] See Cameron Hawley, "Needed: More Tough-Minded Leaders in Business," *Personnel*, May-June, 1960, pp. 55–58.

and briefings that for all practical purposes the executive was worse off than before.

Business is learning that in a system already steeped in bureaucracy, subdivision enhances bureaucracy more than it helps individual initiative. Decentralization and perhaps many future programs concerned with restoring executive initiative fail because the men given the additional authority do not have the competence and confidence to execute that responsibility. Therefore, decentralization has been followed by recentralization above and the mushrooming of bureaucrats below.

Many critics of bureaucracy fear that business enterprise will cease to grow. But even this charge is not yet justified because passing through the decentralization-recentralization cycle has not impeded growth even with the increased bureaucracy. The fact is that bureaucracy has made possible further and more rationally planned growth. Executives today are greatly optimistic that there is, after all, no limit to the size that an enterprise can reach. No one individual really needs to control an enterprise or could control it if he wanted to. It is managed by countless numbers of functionaries whose expertese, constrained by over-all directives, is the basis of controlled integrated action.

The bureaucratic theme is probably stronger in the executive role today than at any other time. We shall now examine some of the bureaucratic phenomena in administration. Not all bureaucrats possess all the qualities described. For example, Donald Clinton Power, chairman and chief executive of General Telephone and Electronics Corporation, the large independent telephone system, runs his corporation as quietly and efficiently as a college classroom. On the one hand, he practices routine regularity in many respects, including keeping

nine to five hours and poring over minute facts logically and
dispassionately; on the other hand, he issues few memos and
calls few meetings. His is a tidy bureaucracy in many respects,
but it also contains wide areas of freedom for subordinates.

The bureaucrat will be discussed in extreme form. However,
except on paper, the bureaucrat may be hard to distinguish
from the autocrat. In fact, the bureaucrat may be described as
a systematic autocrat.

The Systematic Orientation

The bureaucrat accepts his role as one who puts himself and
others into narrowly prescribed roles. He excels at developing
skilled individuals who maximize their collective efforts
through highly rational and formal relationships. It is not
necessary for him to know the rationality of the total program,
but only that part in which his expertese is expressed.

Basic to the systematic orientation is the view that any
program that only autocrats or men of uninhibited emotions
can administer is a dangerous trap of inefficiency and irresponsibility. Maximum effectiveness is found in the routinization of performance through expertese that is not the property
of any single individual. The autocrat's desire to become competent in all things is a basic cause of inefficiency and chaos.
No one should strive to become a generalist, because a broad
competency is subject to error and abuse. The specialist represents the proper way of life because he is orderly directed
toward precision and efficiency.

When one develops an administrative format based on the
concept of specialization, the eventual tendency is to reduce
variations in skill to predictable proportions. Thus, the major
tendency is to consider the expertese and not the expert. The
skill rather than the person is valued. In other words, the office

determines the man rather than the man determines the office. If the man determines the office, the organization becomes overdetermined by the efforts of one man. If he is whimsical or remiss there are few safeguards to prevent catastrophe. When an administrative format encompasses the efforts of numerous individuals, the possibility of error is in inverse proportion to the number of individuals involved in the problem.

Continuity is achieved because the system is greater than any one individual. His absence or relief will not affect the whole system functionally. Furthermore, replacement of individuals takes place effectively because positions are not distorted by the aggressive and unique qualities of an autocrat who seldom can be replaced.

But more fundamentally, the bureaucrat feels that individuals as such cannot be trusted. They may be arbitrary or subject to the wrong influences. But whatever the case, their personal assumption of responsibility will endanger unity and central goal achievement. Just recently this was illustrated in the U-2 incident. The left hand was undoing the work of the right hand, because both were allowed to act on the basis of their own definition of responsibility.

The bureaucrat feels that by locking individuals into a functionally integrated system, the problems of trust and irresponsibility are obviated. This concept is illustrated by a brochure called *Systemation*, put out for advertisement by a consulting company that makes a good living selling bureaucracy to executives. Here are two of the catchy statements aimed at the executive who is overwhelmed by his responsibilities. "Good systems tend to restrict people enough to ensure good teamwork." "Put life into your procedures by putting people into them." Notice that the emphasis is on a basic distrust of the individual per se and the need to put him into a tight, pre-determined system.

The autocrat cannot divide broad complex administrative problems into box-like areas of responsibility. In fact, he is more apt to stimulate performance and vigor by building over-lapping functions and responsibilities into his administrative format.

Furthermore, he likes to make rules to accommodate specific situations and then change them when he feels they are no longer necessary, thus keeping a fluid administrative base. He assumes responsibility for adjusting it to meet changing circumstances. For this he is willing to stand alone and make solitary decisions.

The bureaucrat cannot conceive of himself in a solitary capacity. He needs support around him, but it is not the group to which he turns. Decisions are made by consulting precedent, rules, and procedures. If these fail, other experts may be consulted and a problem may be moved to higher authority. He does not view group processes as essential to bureaucracy, for the formal group is inefficient and awkward. It lacks order, precision, and predictability. It often fails to act, elicits unnecessary problems in personal relationships, and is basically irresponsible. It may be useful as a device for training people and for gathering information, but should not be used authoritatively or habitually. The bureaucrat's concept of team is found in each individual playing his separate role as an integrated part of the whole. The system is the bureaucrat's unit of authority and control.

The systematic orientation is, therefore, based upon sequential relationships rather than individual units of performance. It is the pattern or structure of their several contributions that is crucial to over-all performance. Consequently, the systematic orientation is prone to cast nonarranged affairs into a sequential order. The bureaucrat's skill lies in making order out of unstructured relationships. In so doing he creates a well-structured environment in which to operate comfortably. This is the ultimate of the putting-in tendency. The bureaucrat builds a bureau for every one of his subordinates, including one for himself, into which he drops safely, never to return again voluntarily to the ambiguity of life in the open and unbounded.

In this regard the difference between the autocrat and bureaucrat is clearly seen. The autocrat is a man of action who overwhelms and overresponds. He is a dynamic man of power who destroys all obstacles in his environment. The bureaucrat meets these obstacles with a preconceived plan about how these objects may be related. To control them means that they must be moved about into the proper arrangement, which requires attention to their logical relationships.

The difference between the autocrat and bureaucrat shows most clearly in matters of administrative reform. Experts today are called upon to ponder the ills of federal governmental agencies. These agencies are bureaucratically stalled in sluggish, costly, meaningless practices based upon rules and regulations that offer no adequate prospect for the future. Executives in these agencies have let matters drift, ignored the public interest, and failed to make policy pronouncements. James M. Landis was asked to give a report on what needs to be done. His recommendation was to get better men to make the weak structure work. This view happens to be a clear example of the autocrat's approach to administrative reform.

Louis J. Herter defined the issue in Congressional testimony in a typically bureaucratic manner. He saw the issue as arising from basic and inescapable contradictions in the structural relationships of the agencies. Like a typical bureaucrat, he recommended that the structure be revised and realigned, mainly to take policy-making from the agencies and transfer it to the executive branch. His reasoning is not difficult to follow in terms of the bureaucratic view. Policy and execution are two entirely different functional activities and should therefore be separated structurally. Naturally, this recommendation is made irrespective of the men involved who actually occupy the agency or will in the future.

Landis's major emphasis is on the need for better men who can make the present laws and rules work. Herter answers that our regulating machinery must be able to run with less than dynamic men operating it. "The federal courts run well with great judges and ordinary judges." Round and round goes the argument today. It is clear that the bureaucrat is oriented toward proper functional relationships integrated around a rationalized set of goals. The autocrat sees the individual, his ability to take charge and get the job done in spite of the difficulties, as the unit of his administrative format. The one seeks to rearrange and the other to overpower.

The Tidy Show Complex

The systematic orientation inevitably develops a need for tidiness in both personal and administrative areas. Generally the bureaucrat abhors messy situations. Field Marshal Montgomery showed this tendency in World War II. Eisenhower writes, "Montgomery was always a master in the methodical preparation of forces for a formal, set-piece attack."[5] He never did appreciate the American desire to keep pressing forward, shifting their men, and recombining on the attack. Said Montgomery, "You must have a well balanced, tidy show when you

[5] Dwight D. Eisenhower, *Crusade in Europe*, Doubleday, 1948, p. 428.

are mixed up in a dog fight. . . . You can't win the big victory without a tidy show."[6]

Montgomery could not operate effectively without structural tidiness. His eccentric "putting-in" tendency separated him habitually from his staff. He lived in a trailer and refused to be awakened from his sleep no matter what the extent of the crisis. He consistently refused to deal with staff officers from any headquarters other than his own. "In argument he was persistent up to the point of decision."[7]

In some executives the desire for a tidy show is passive and may be expressed only during lulls in activity. He may merely be interested in sprucing up his administrative format and may tinker with an improvement in his communications or evaluation system. However, the executive who holds strongly to the bureaucratic approach is compelled to keep a tidy show as a condition of executive competence. He is upset when he is in the midst of a messy situation.

Cleanliness may be expressed personally by housekeeping procedures. To him dirt is matter in the wrong place or out of place. He will keep his desk immaculately clean. His office may have a planned look with everything in perfect array. Ash trays next to each chair, magazines neatly arranged on a table next to the door or his desk, telephone inside his desk, and desk glass meticulously shined. He may insist upon the same personal neatness in his people, especially his secretary.

Or he may insist on procedural cleanliness with no wasted motion by him or anyone. People are there when they are needed, doing exactly what is required of them with no unusual episodes of loud talking or emotional strain.

Still further, he may insist on administrative cleanliness.

[6] John Toland, *Battle: The Story of the Bulge*, Random House, 1959, p. 48.
[7] Eisenhower, *op. cit.*, p. 322.

He may want clean, precise lines of authority and responsibility, everyone in the right niche, doing the proper thing with no overlapping and no incompatibility. Such a view of an administrative format is akin to a mechanical concept of a smoothly running engine with no noises and inefficiency. The system is in perfect adjustment with its purpose.

One cannot avoid comparing the bureaucrat with Roosevelt on this point of administrative tidiness. Stimson often said that he had no system. He scattered responsibility among many uncoordinated men. He hopped erratically from one department to another to do another department's work. "I doubt," said Stimson, "whether we shall be able to hold him to any very systematic relations because that is rather entirely antithetic to his nature and temperament." One authority observed, "Roosevelt's normal way of organizing a department was to split it right down the middle. He encouraged such a duplication of effort, an overlapping of authorities and a development of personal antagonisms that in some cases they amounted almost to civil war."[8] Roosevelt was a master at making messy situations and turning them into administrative advantages.

A tidy show gives the bureaucrat the feeling that he is competent or doing a competent job, and it also makes him a reliable object to deal with. His personal and procedural relationships create a well-delineated set of expectations. Thus, in a large or complex office situation he may be a stabilizing factor.

When his need for a tidy show is erratic the result may be different. There are some bureaucrats who revert to a tidy show sequence when entering a threatening situation or a

[8] See Ernest R. May, ed., *The Ultimate Decision*, Braziller, 1960, pp. 135–180.

crisis. In such a case the executive may spend considerable time tidying the office or re-establishing a rule with the telephone operator about when not to interrupt his privacy. What prevents the erratic style from being completely disturbing is that, after observing his reactions to crisis, subordinates will begin to shift with him to a different set of expectations, depending upon his mood. The bureaucrat may be rescued indirectly from his difficulty by the flexibility of his own subordinates.

Usually the tidy show sequence does not become generalized throughout the whole executive pattern. It is focused on several specific attributes that usually aid the executive's approach to problems. This seldom destroys his effectiveness. But when it becomes generalized to a point that his day may be ruined because some trivial element messed up what otherwise would have been a clean situation, then profound disturbances are created in his relationships.

Regularity

Regularity, another element of the bureaucratic style, is an outgrowth of the need to practice personal or administrative cleanliness. It is basically punctuality. To have people straggling into a conference at different times is a kind of messy situation. The bureaucrat strictly observes appointed times. He is never late and would rather be early. But preferably he is on time, neither early nor late. He may get up at the same time each morning, be at the breakfast table at the same time, and be in the office at the stroke of nine. If he conforms closely to the bureaucratic style, he will leave at the stroke of five, not staying to work late because there are other schedules in the evening for him to follow punctually.

A case in point is Donald Douglas, president of Douglas

Aircraft, who attacks his problems with a passion for perfection and precision. He clocks his own activities rigidly and never has a wasted moment or fails to take advantage of a free moment. He is always on time.

A punctuality pattern is one of a high degree of routine. It implies a need to be methodically aware of the space-time features of a day. At a certain time the bureaucrat should be at a certain place; it may be expected of him and his subordinates to have coffee in the company cafeteria at ten o'clock, lunch at noon, and Coke at three. For example, so strictly were Campbell Soup Company executives expected to fit a routine that until recently vice-presidents had to notify the president if they planned to be away from the office, even to go to the dentist. A former ad man describes Revlon, only half in jest, as "a place if you come to work late, you bring a letter of excuse from your parents." Of course, there are many examples of the current insistence on punctuality and routine regularity.

The bureaucrat punctuates his day sequence with events which seem to direct his behavior. The more routine these events are, the more they conform to his desire, and he will resist having them tampered with. For example, many executives will not schedule conferences the first hour of the day because during this time they begin to ease into the routine of the day. They open their mail, check on correspondence, and line themselves up with their schedule, which hopefully is not different from any other day.

Because the bureaucrat tends to view his day as a series of punctuated efforts, he may very well favor setting unplanned events at specific times. Some executives think of conferences as morning affairs, some as afternoon, while others consider them to be luncheon affairs. Visitors are often encouraged to go to lunch to avoid disturbing the orderly sequence of the day's events. Of course, routine becomes an attempt to develop distinct patterns of clearly predictable relationships. The executive may always go to lunch with the same individual or group, talk to the same colleague about his problems, or develop a conference routine among his subordinates for a given kind of administrative problem.

For policy formulation executives will frequently call upon different colleagues and subordinates from those called upon for execution activities. The roles played under these two circumstances will be different but not unpredictably so. There is nothing quite as disturbing to the bureaucrat as calling a policy meeting that is attended by an individual who plays the wrong role.

Routine regularity is also found in the attempt to routinize the behavior of the executive's subordinates. By developing clearly defined duties the bureaucrat is able to keep people in predictable relationships. Any error is then quickly recognized, the responsibility allocated, and the discipline fairly instituted. Unroutinized activity cannot be controlled since by its very essence it involves spontaneity on the part of the subordinate.

The bureaucrat tends to believe that spontaneity is the cause of much inefficiency. It is not that he should eliminate it entirely; this is neither possible nor desirable. But he does attempt to control it by routinizing the operations of some subordinates and, at the same time, allowing a few subordinates the opportunity to break set. These individuals are singled out along some objectively recognized criterion, such as performance or skill. They are given loosely controlled duties which have built-in opportunities for diversity. These jobs, however, defy routinization and are established by the bureaucrat only to control the need for spontaneity, not to allow free expression of it. If he had his way, there would be no room for impulsive, spontaneous, and creative behavior among his subordinates.

Of course, some bureaucrats are not aware of the need to limit routinized regularity to those duties and positions that lend themselves to close control. They attempt to routinize where routine regularity is a travesty of the essence of the function or position. In such cases retaliatory practices must always be resorted to in order to bring events into line with expectations. Crises are common when artificial routinization is imposed where it cannot hope to succeed.

A crisis in a bureaucracy is no small thing. In fact, every small, unplanned event is a potential crisis. The crisis necessarily involves the executive himself. Since he must interrupt his routine, he is determined to resolve it forever. After a thorough examination of every possible detail, including events that are only peripherally related, procedures are laid down to avoid a similar occurrence. The bureaucrat returns to his routine, hopeful that nothing will distract him from his pattern again for a while.

Accuracy

The tidy show complex and regularity both support the bureaucratic element of reliability. The whole bureaucratic scheme depends on being free of error. A reliable administrative format is the same as a reliable formula. Satisfactory results may be expected with complete confidence. Consequently, each individual must be worthy of being trusted and believed in.

The major sin in a bureaucracy is questionable, deceitful, and undependable behavior. One can easily see why. Vast programs minutely broken down into routinized sequences can achieve integration only by each individual fulfilling his duties. Although each individual has duties that are to him insignificant, he must not view them as such. However, the fact that each duty seems immaterial to the performance of the whole is in itself a temptation to be unreliable.

The unspoken corollary is, "Figures don't lie." The typical bureaucrat feels it is easier and safer to obtain summaries from facts and figures than it is from people directly. People are not prone to fudge on what they put down on paper as they are in unrecorded conversation. The bureaucrat places naïve faith in the written word. Every now and then he is startled by the disrespect that others might show for the printed word. Khrushchev recently discovered that a subordinate in the great grain-producing Ukraine had lied about corn production. "I am sure," Khrushchev declared, "that the figures you give are only half the harvest and the other half was stolen in the field." "You are right," replied Podgorny, whereupon he got a tongue lashing. Khrushchev made less noise about the fudging than about the low corn production. A more bureaucratic type would not have gotten past fuming about the fudging of figures, so terribly dependent is he upon reports for his administrative style.

Consequently, the bureaucrat establishes a reporting system of three- and four-copy depth not only to keep others informed, but also to hold the individual to his task at hand. Reports become so important that the subordinate must often spend considerable time and energy in their preparation. They become red tape—a condition in which secondary responsibilities set up to insure the working of a primary endeavor get in the way of that endeavor. For example, during the war in one large naval air unit, the most trivial correspondence was routed up to the chief of staff and often to the admiral, then down to the appropriate department for action. The reply was drafted and typed, routed back to the top for approval and signature, which were often refused pending minor changes, and finally routed down to the dispatching office. Mail which a clerk should have handled in and out in twenty-four hours was thus sent to the top and back two or three times, drawing attention from eight to twelve persons over a ten-day period.[9]

Accurate reports are so essential that the bureaucrat places major emphasis on the job of getting them in on time from subordinates. His creative effort is directed toward finding better ways of receiving and assessing reports from his staff. Furthermore, because of the emphasis on accurate reports, he cannot avoid basing most of his appraisal of the effective working of the total system on these reports. This leads also to appraising his subordinate's performance by means of the report system. The public image of the bureaucrat sitting in his office running a vast system from his desk is correct. He is a paper shuffler and thrives on this characteristic of his administrative style.

Reliance on accurate reports requires a system of preserving them for future reference. This means that eventually the bureaucrat turns his thoroughness to contriving a file system that classifies everything by subject, date, and reply. Nothing can be as crucial to maintaining an accurate report system as keeping accurate tabs on what was said before about what subject. This allows not only thorough analysis of the effect of past events on present difficulties, but also evaluation of the consistency, reliability, and honesty of the individual in question. Some bureaucrats rely so heavily upon their file system that they alone hold the keys to the locks and only under extreme conditions will they part with them.

[9] Joseph Bensman and Bernard Rosenberg, "The Meaning of Work in Bureaucratic Society," in Maurice Stein, ed., *Identity and Anxiety*, Free Press, 1960, p. 189.

Of course, all communication of any significance must be put in writing. This helps keep an accurate file of an individual's contribution as well as his promises or obligations. In many cases an informal conversation which bears the possibility of a formal assignment will be interrupted so as to bring in a secretary to record the conversation. This need for everything in writing decreases even more the bureaucrat's face-to-face contact with his subordinates, which in turn breeds more of the same—more written reports.

The Ritual of Rules

Conscientiousness in the performance of petty duties is an ingredient in the bureaucratic style, but the autocrat loves to submerge himself in details too. However, he is impulsive, unpredictable, and sloppy, while the bureaucrat practices detail immersion with orderly, predictable vengeance. Furthermore, the autocrat will freely violate his own executive pattern, whereas the bureaucrat will not violate his rules and regulations even if they were largely his own creation.

Because rules and regulations are essential in keeping the whole system together in working order, they cannot be violated without incurring risk. To the autocrat rules are to bind his subordinates, but to the bureaucrat they are to bind all, including himself and mostly himself. He must set the example. Strong sentiments buttress the ideal of loyally serving rules and regulations. The bureaucrat comes to identify both his competence and his self-respect with his strict observance of rules. Rules rule the self.

This system of sentiment gives status and self-respect to those who conform exactly to the rules and directives. Great pleasure is obtained from being able to cite a rule or directive which someone failed to observe or remember. Even if the rule-breaker is unwillfully errant, it may be difficult for him to feel comfortable and for others to show him sympathy. So strong are the sentiments against rule-breaking that effective discipline is accomplished by the efforts of each individual with a minimum control from the superior. In this respect the bureaucratic style is different from the autocratic, which depends upon unilateral control from a sole authority.

In extreme bureaucracy there is a tendency for the observance of rules and regulations to become a ritualistic activity, even to a point where concern with conformity to the rules interferes with achievement of the purposes of the organization. The result is another example of red tape—the arbitrary adherence to some technicality that is convenient but irrelevant.

In this ritualistic phase of bureaucracy, secondary rules or means become primary ends in themselves. Rules become symbolic rather than utilitarian, displacing the original purpose for which they were intended. Thus the very elements of the bureaucratic style which are conducive to efficiency in general may produce inefficiency. The bureaucrat must discover where efficiency ends and inefficiency begins. When emotional attitudes become attached to the observance of rules the objectivity required for appreciating their limitations is lost.

Impersonality and Vindictiveness

With the loss of objectivity due to ritualistic observance of rules the bureaucrat becomes impersonal. The sacred adoption of rules means unreserved submission to them. They take on a kind of moral character that displaces the superego of the individual. By the observance of rules he is not only a better functionary, but a better person.

The rules give him an opportunity to achieve a sense of

importance and propriety. The more petty the rules the greater the feeling of importance when they are observed. Genuine involvement with reality in the outer world is precluded by overidentification with rules. For example, Nazi documents, captured after World War II, show that on the day Hitler took his own life in a bunker in Berlin and Russian troops were filling the streets, officials of the Reichschancellery were too busy to look out their windows. "They were engaged in estimating and ordering paper clips for the next fiscal year."[10]

This detachment allows the bureaucrat to give impersonal treatment to colleagues or clients whose needs are to them quite crucial and personal. When dealing with the public such impersonality may appear as arrogance or haughtiness. Bureaucrats in charity organizations may appear almost beyond the reach of human sympathy. They have been known to grant or withhold life sustaining benefits with a degree of impersonality that borders on schizophrenia.

The bureaucrat can maintain this impersonality because of his feeling of superiority when acting in submission to rules. His sense of power derives from his identification with the ideal bureaucratic style. Consequently, there are strong inner urges to prevent showing any personality in the bureaucratic role. Usually when an individual fails to meet these expectations, conflict occurs not only in himself but with others who are sociably and emotionally impersonal and immune to his individualized needs.

The sophisticated bureaucrat may wrap up his ego further by imputing human attributes to his organization. For example, he views it as a living organism that extends beyond the life of any one person, including himself. At his worst he

[10] *Ibid.*, p. 189.

feels himself a cog; at his best he feels himself a runner in a relay race.

Contrariwise, the man of action, the autocrat, resists losing himself this way and conceives of the enterprise more within the orbit of certain goals that can be definitely accomplished by the application of his energy. For this reason change in autocrats is often followed by major changes in personnel and organization. Change in bureaucrats usually means more of the same bureaucracy.

Bureaucratic style almost always evidences the element of obstinacy, which, at times, may develop into defiance of superior authority. A bureaucrat's pride may be easily offended. He is proud of his executive style, but at the same time in conflict with it. He is aware that colleagues, customers, clients, or the public may regard him as a "noninteger," an impersonal cog in the wheel. Because of his awareness of what others think of his style, he is driven all the more into it. He must exhibit pride, even if it is for the purpose of showing conviction and satisfaction with his role. Thus, neurotic pride grows from a need to support a role that inherently lacks profound experiences. Irascibility over minor offenses may become vindictiveness when this neurotic pride cannot be exhibited without the use of the authority and expertese of his role.

Bureaucratic vindictiveness becomes domination of another by the meticulous enforcement of rules. Once this pattern is set, there is little escape for the offender except through appeal to a higher authority or complete submission to the bureaucrat himself. Bureaucrats know how to make others squirm when they are denied expression of dignity and pride. They may become classical obstructionists with the complete support of the system itself. They may become almost insurmountable if they choose. The bureaucracy is anchored around a system of informal cliques that operate to constrain common enemies and support common friends. Such an informal system can come together at a moment's notice to place a superior's position in jeopardy.

Bureaucrats have been known to withhold adequate information, overload the information channels, and in general make the objective problems of an uncooperative boss or colleague so difficult that the only alternatives are to exit or to give total submission. And all of this can be achieved without any apparent evidence of collusion. This element of vindictiveness has accounted for the failure of many secretaries of defense who were too naïve about the nature of the bureaucratic complex in the Pentagon.

Vindictiveness and collusion make the system immune to changes from without. The autocrat who inherits a bureaucratic system has little choice but to go along with it in the main. His opportunity for self-rule is nil.

The Magic of Words

Words become very important to the bureaucrat. First, he must write many reports to satisfy the need for accuracy, and second, the specialized jargon of his expertese serves an important function in keeping his behavior orderly and precise. As adjustment to his role increases the bureaucrat acquires a very cautious approach to the solution of problems. He begins to feel that he must anticipate possible problems and consequences that might arise from behavior not clearly authorized by established rules and directives. Rather than act immediately he will use words, whether in a report or just in talking out a problem, in an attempt to anticipate. Success with this use of words reinforces the substitution of words for immediate action. If he is not successful, that is, if he does not anticipate consequences or if his report or suggestions meet with disapproval, he may become even more cautious, and therefore rely even more heavily on the use of words.

Words become "magic helpers." If he is afraid to follow a course of action, he may write it up in a report to be conveniently put away in his file or in the wastepaper basket. Some bureaucrats have vast orderly files of changes they once contemplated. To avoid actions that frighten and threaten him, he flees from the world of things and actions to the world of words and reports. If the words inside files were ever translated into action, the whole system would have to be changed, and therefore they must simply be filed away.

This belief in words may be related to childhood experiences in which the frightening aspects of the world seem to be mastered by giving them names. In infancy words are magical and omnipotent, they can kill and resurrect, they can perform miracles and turn back time. In the adult, reason, words, and thoughts as well as action must be handled cautiously.

Bureaucratic thought processes lead to emphasizing thinking about acting rather than acting. The bureaucrat claims that thinking is the preparation for action and is justified because it aims at making action efficient. But because of the tremendous risks in action, the bureaucrat type may prefer thinking to acting, and thereby prepare constantly for the future and never experience the present. Busy with preparations, he acts according to the rule that the status quo is better than anything a change might bring. The status quo is a lesser evil. Much effort and time is dissipated in resorting to words because change is not feasible.

The Bu-Reactor

Although the bureaucrat clings to his system with religious fervor, every once in a while a severe reaction sets in against it, as though he suddenly sees the trap and attempts a last minute extrication. This "bu-reaction" is almost always accompanied by a burst of emotional vitality directed against the ends of the system. A bu-reactor stands within the bureaucracy shouting about getting out, but never really making any attempt to get out. His shouting against it is in direct proportion to his desire to stay in his bureaucratic box.

Companies with many high-level bu-reactors have been known to go through cataclysmic eruptions in the form of devastating reshuffling of the administrative personnel. Charges of indecisivness, red tape, conservatism fly around; some people are severely accused of actually being bureaucrats. Oddly enough a few do lose their positions because the label is successfully attached to them. Finding these scapegoats allows the bu-reactor to vent his fears and anxieties. He can then return to his bureaucratic style, feeling that he is not really a bureaucrat after all. At a later date another bu-reaction may set in for the same purposes and with the same results. Some always get hurt, but those who stay feel cleaner and more competent.

The bu-reactor is quite common today. In fact, he is in style. He performs properly with the bureaucratic qualities of precision, reliability, and efficiency. But he is incapable of maintaining a consistent pattern with these elements. He talks aggressively about how he constantly looks for opportunities to be creative and spontaneous. He may even attempt to be a little creative or spontaneous, though never in a hazardous way, of course. In meetings and conferences he injects notions of change and diversity and the human or administrative need for flexibility and individuality.

In many respects the bu-reactor is part of what Durkheim called the "cult of individual personality." It is important to be different from other people, not in order to develop one's special talents for the good of society, but as a ritual practiced from fear of relying too much on established rules and regulations. The bu-reactor assiduously adopts variations in his routine and procedures in order to cover up his total dependence upon the system. He has a flair for being uncommonly common.

The bu-reactor achieves a sense of prestige and identity by ranting judiciously against the system. Yet he violates none of the sacred rituals and taboos. Although he is not functionally vulnerable, he achieves the appearance of wholesome independence and is therefore able to go on being a bureaucrat. Guilt feelings are assuaged by his self-critical confession. Little does he realize that even his confession is a bureaucratic element. It becomes a routine with him to the point that certain key words, individuals, or situations trigger his bu-reaction.

A bu-reactor often has no effect in bringing about a general bu-reaction in the organization. In fact, by his release of tension, he may aid in controlling a general reaction against the system and preventing a cataclysmic eruption of antibureaucratic tendencies. If a superior does not allow bu-reactors to give their routine confessions he paves the way for a generalized rebellion, for the antibureaucratic feelings will be given expression sometime and somehow. He can do a lot at strategic times by playing the role of a bu-reactor himself. By airing occasional complaints about the "system," he can encourage or restrain expression of these emotions by others, and thereby control them. However, if he does allow bu-reactors to express themselves, they may eventually offend his authority and power. He must therefore maintain the proper balance between expression and repression.

The evil of the bu-reactor is that he prevents real change. Members of the organization may refer to "new" rules and "new" directives which are not new at all. The game is often to go along with slight technical changes to accommodate the bu-reactive ideal.

In conclusion, bureaucracy strongly attracts those who achieve productivity and security by immersion in an intricate and exact system of functional responsibilities. The dangers are great. The executive must support the needs of bureaucracy or forfeit the advantages that are provided by systematic endeavor. He must serve and master the forces that bombard the executive role.

But bureaucracy is almost impossible for many to resist and master. It makes subtle inroads into the personality. It is best illustrated by the experiment in physiology in which a frog can be unknowingly boiled alive by gradually and imperceptibly raising the temperature of the water. Bureaucracy is not a cataclysmic eruption, but a petrification which is determined by how many rules are instituted without conscious awareness of their presence. Change usually means more bureaucracy.

The executive who tends to seek refuge in bounded roles and functions will be easily mesmerized. Executives have been known to sneer at their supposed bureaucratic mesmerization while at the same time they display preoccupation with trivia and concern for feasibility before consideration of desirability. Little do they realize that their unconscious adaptation to bureaucracy attests to the genius of that system and not its lack of presence.

For many of them the awareness does not come until they reach top policy-making positions. Here they may realize how severely diminished are the intellectual and emotional qualities they need for formulation of broad objectives and programs. They cannot become superior to the system when they most desperately need to be. The tragedy is that they emerge at the top stunted personalities, incapable of moving without complete assurance and unwilling to incur risk.

Their number is fantastically large today. Unfortunately, they are among those businessmen who are going out into the community to perform public service. Their "trained incapacity," as some call it, works its harm in institutions heretofore preserved from the lethargy of the systematic orientation. In the attempt to save the world from disorderliness, the bureaucrat may install subtle tyranny.

CHAPTER 7

THE DEMOCRAT

The democratic style is based on the sharing orientation. The democrat practices the art of sharing himself and
his administrative resources with others to the end of individual and organizational welfare. He manifests a deep confidence in the benevolent potentiality of people. This affirmative
trust allows much energy that might be inhibited or turned
inward in the service of the self to be directed outward in the
service of others.

The Meaning of Democracy

Democracy is a term as emotionally loaded as autocracy or
bureaucracy. Often it is not considered a legitimate term of
administration; to administer democracy seems to many to be
a contradiction. Democracy is for them something that results
from an absence of administration. However, the very word
democracy implies the presence of rule, of administration of
some kind. It is not something devoid of activity, and if it is

activity it must also imply control of circumstances and of people. It is a kind of organization.

Democracy comes into being when the activities of people follow their own choices and plans. These choices must be implemented in the manner characteristic of their purpose or intent. There must be order, and to assure order there must be respect for authority and power. Democracy is necessarily occasioned by the coefficients of power and order.

Democracy is acquired through administration. It can also be snuffed out by administration. Executives who are committed to developing and preserving democracy are greatly needed when the tendencies of power and order appear to threaten freedom and spontaneity as they do today. With society as thoroughly organized as it is, the individual most apt to be the effective guardian and promoter of human freedom and dignity is the executive himself. If the values of democracy are successfully preserved and developed, it will be largely due to the work of those who wield the instruments of power and order.

Too often the term democracy is used to mean the end to which all other purposes are subservient, or it is used as a symbol of a sublime and noble ideal. However, it is most meaningful when fused with purposes which democarcy cannot achieve by itself. For example, efficiency is not an automatic result of freedom, but freedom can be either an ally or enemy of efficiency, depending upon how it is administered. This same condition holds for efficiency. The presence of a good procedure does not guarantee justice or equality. Power, order, and freedom may be administratively fused to produce results which cannot be achieved by any one element alone.

In the administrative function democracy adds something

that power and order cannot. Neither power nor order strives to provide freedom. They are basically self-serving and self-sustaining devices unless modified substantially by the affiliative impulses.

When democracy is added to the executive style, power and order are aimed in different directions. The democratic element transforms them. For example, an authoritative request in an autocratic administration may be received as a dictatorial demand. In a democratic administration it may be accepted as an important request. The power inherent in the circumstances may be equivalent in effect, but not similar in character. In one case power has a coercive quality, in the other a representative quality. The one separates the sender and the receiver of the message, the other unites them.

Although all executives are to some degree autocratic, bureaucratic, and democratic, they are more precisely known by the kind of power, order, and love that evolve from their administrative activity. The power that emerges from a predominantly democratic format is not the same in character as that from an autocratic format.

After recognizing these differences in executive styles, it must be stated that power in any format usually amounts to domination of some kind. The question often raised is, "If love is united with power, where are the proper limits of their union?" In other words, where does autocracy conflict with democracy? It conflicts with democracy when it inhibits the purposes of democracy, namely, the tendency of people to achieve through voluntary choice organized behavior directed toward communal ends. By this definition everything that hinders that achievement is working against democracy. If inefficiency or abuse of power is the culprit, it must be obviated or redirected. One tragic aspect of democracy is that, when these conditions are threatened, it may be necessary to use force. While seeking unity, people may become divided.

The Union of the Separated

In general individuals work in their organizations as individuals, that is, as separate units connected by systematic activity. Massive oganization requires that individuals and departments divide and subdivide the performance of single operations. There are times when the individual is not fully aware of the total of which his task is a part. He works only on one phase of a task which is assigned to him by another and relayed upon completion to still another, who carries on in the same blind fashion. Efficiency divides activity into functional units that are performed by specific individuals who take on the mentality of those functional units. They grow to see themselves as separated rather than united. They may be busy with the task at hand, but they are not involved in the planning and conduct of the total work before them.

Power also separates men. Every individual in modern organization knows where he stands structurally, who is above, below, and at his side. By perception and informed guesses each knows whether he is "in" or "out" with people who are able to effect his future career. In either case, power differentials tend to emphasize his essential separateness from others.

Were it not for the various ingredients of democracy, the individual would feel very much alone in the midst of the large number of office and factory workers. Of course, many do feel this loneliness, this separateness. However, the democratic style attempts to unite those separated by the requirements of power and order. The executive does this by attempting to share the things that separate people, namely, power and expertese. He shares his power, skills, beliefs, and interests; his

problems, assignments, and responsibilities. He shares the resources available to him through his administrative function
and his personal capacity. Through mutual participation the
separateness may be greatly overcome. The democratic style
makes power and order tolerable, gives them purpose and
meaning, reduces their coercive effects. The terms appropriate
here are team spirit, group cohesiveness. A case in point is
Harmon S. Eberhard, president of Caterpillar Tractor Company, who was chosen by his predecessor, Mr. Neumiller,
primarily because the latter saw him as "one of the most
selfless individuals I've met." His reputation is well described
in his own words. "My job is trying to help others do their
best. " By his unselfish sharing of himself Eberhard was able to
build an effective cohesive team.

There are many burlesque translations of how to create
team spirit. Mr. McDonnell of McDonnell Aircraft Corporation in St. Louis blurts out through a public address system
information and pleasantries to keep his 27,000 workers
abreast of important company views. "This is Mac calling all
personnel; this is Mac calling the Team." Mr. McDonnell is
typical of executives who annually toss millions of dollars and
uncounted time and effort into company picnics, staff news-
letters, executive luncheons, stock option plans, employee
hobby clubs, weekend meetings at resorts, theatre parties, informal dinners or cocktail parties, fishing trips, and golf out-
ings. Corporate boosters continually pound home "The
Team," or as it is known in cozier companies, "The family."[1]

However, these tricks and fads do not unite people for the
simple reason that what separates people is not in the least
changed. The systems of power and expertese are what divide,
and unless they are changed to accommodate human ambi-

---

[1] *The Wall Street Journal*, November 13, 1957, p. 14.

tions, no amount of company picnics will build a united people. They will be united in name only. The genuine democrat does not attempt to unite people upon bases that are incidental to the causes of their feelings of loneliness and insignificance.

Also, the true democrat knows that the separated individuals must not be united at the cost of losing their identity, for this would ignore the essential quality of freedom. If individuals are engulfed there can be no true union.

Eisenhower may have lacked certain qualities that people want in an administrator, but he did not lack this capacity to unite the most antagonistic personalities under the same roof without destroying their identities. Secretary of Defense Charles E. Wilson's foot-in-mouth troubles were similar to those suffered by General George S. Patton when he was in General Eisenhower's command. In each case Eisenhower was annoyed by the commotion but did not take punitive action because he respected them and felt each was particularly fitted by character and experience to do the job assigned. Similarly, Eisenhower saw the value of the combination of General John C. H. Lee, commander of American logistics organization in the European campaign. "I was ready to waive the rigidity of his mannerisms in favor of his constructive qualities. Indeed, I felt it possible that his unyielding methods might be vital in an activity where an iron hand is always mandatory."[2]

In each of these cases, Eisenhower effectively united basically rigid and antisocial personalities without the loss of their individuality. He had an uncommon ability to administer democracy and to achieve compromise, minimize frictions, and obtain teamwork among conflicting interests and people without imposing his will by harsh command.

[2] Eisenhower, *op. cit.*, p. 267.

The crucial point is that an individual may acquire identity through his capacity to engage in mutual relationships. The quality of this interaction, acting upon his inherent disposition, makes him the person he is.

Some people come to their administrative responsibility rather well equipped to share in mutual relationships. Others come poorly equipped. Their inability to engage in meaningful human relationships does not allow them to include genuine elements of the democratic style in their administrative format. They feel separated and alone while wanting to be loved and united.

To achieve their aims they may pervert the concept of democracy by overwhelming others with acts of kindness and sympathy. They may be oversolicitous, erratically kind, and demonstratively affectionate. While they attempt to produce good human relations, their subordinates find themselves unable to move or breathe. They may not get angry because their bosses are so diligent and dedicated, nor can they be indifferent because the bosses are apt to feel rebuffed. They feel sat upon by overly responsive parents who for all practical purposes are smothering them to death.

The genuine form of democracy is rooted in the capacity to achieve a sense of association with mankind. This capacity is not an idealistic abstraction to be talked and read about in religious or romantic moods. The executive who must pursue a perverted style of democracy does so because he lacks a central feeling for all men. Because he cannot feel this unity, he cannot seek out those relationships that achieve unity with his superior, subordinates, and peers. His only recourse is to determine the condition of his relationship to them. If he shows affection, he does so on his own terms and at his own request. It is turned on and off as his feelings of loneliness rise and fall. Not knowing for sure which way he will act the next moment, he cannot be sure of who he really is. He fails to provide others and to achieve for himself the identity that may be found only in the capacity to engage in mutually satisfying human relationships.

Equality

The administrative act of sharing is predicated upon the concept of equality. Every individual is capable of feeling united with others or separated from them. Administrative practice based on the concept of equality allows each man to express his capacity for feeling united with others. Many cannot adequately express this need for unity, partly because they have not been taught to relate to others through this need to feel equal. They may have developed a hierarchical orientation that categorizes people as weak or strong, above or below, good or bad. For the autocrat, this either-or complex allows rigid classification of people that serves both his administrative needs to control and psychological needs to dominate. Without this hierarchical view his drive for power would be relatively ineffective.

On the other hand, if the autocrat did not need to feel above or below, he would not perhaps feel the urge to acquire power. Rigid categorization prevents people from accepting each other on a mutual basis and inequality becomes the basis of human relationships. For the autocrat inequality is the primary basis of control. His efforts essentially divide rather than unify people. He would define equality as uniformity, and thus all individual differences, inequality in his terms, are considered as deviation and bad. Here then the concept of equality is construed to deny individual differences.

Crucial to the administration of democracy is the recognition that equality is not uniformity. Rather, equality is sympathetic to true superiority. A superior talent or skill is potentially beneficial to everyone. If it is released to others regardless of their superficial differences, it becomes a strong force for equality.

If the executive is a truly superior person, he will not be averse to sharing his skills and abilities with his superiors, subordinates, and peers. When an individual feels superior only in his position or responsibility, he is apt to rely upon these differences as a way to deal with people. He must keep his subordinates from acting as equals to him, and they must remain equal to one another. He suppresses superiority among them.

When the executive can successfully implement an equalitarian orientation, the effect is sometimes electric. When Fred Emmerich took over Allied Chemical he expressed the equality orientation by remarking with sincerity, "We don't know the answers," and "We're anxious to learn." Emmerich expressed in this statement the idea that he could not run Allied by himself. He needed help and he asked for it. "His vice presidents caught the cue, division heads soon heard the word, and down toward the plants rippled the news that expression of opinions was welcome. The effect was so overwhelming that company executives found themselves making innovations that had been, all along, the obvious things to do.[3] The act of seeking help from subordinates as though they were in fact peers is a key element of the equalitarian orientation. Not everyone is capable of performing in this role.

The equalitarian orientation opens new channels for the discovery and use of talent. The democrat does not tend to classify people big or small, important or unimportant, over

[3] E. L. Van Duesen, "You'd Hardly Know Allied Chemical," *Fortune*, 1954, pp. 119–177.

or under, bad or good. Nor are they all seen as equal by a standard of mediocrity or commonness. Crawford Greenewalt, President of du Pont and an enthusiast of administrative democracy, says, "When people are allowed to sacrifice identity in the damp laundry of mediocrity all of society suffers."

The democrat sees people as individuals, each with different needs. He sees individual differences rather than individual similarities. When only similarities are looked for, true differences are leveled and mediocrity becomes the standard of equality. The equalitarian orientation is rooted in a willingness to recognize and respect all people for their particular needs and strengths. Some of the same qualities that the autocrat sees in people will be seen by the democrat. He may see in some the need to achieve power and in others the need to achieve order. He is more apt to see the autocrat and bureaucrat for what they are and to help them in their different ways than they are to recognize and respect him.

The democrat's equalitarian view also serves both his personal and administrative needs. Feelings of equality allow him to identify readily with superior and subordinates as individuals. He establishes a kind of brotherhood in which each individual is accepted on the merit of his membership in the organization. Differences of need and competency are important, but not differences of dress, rank, prestige, or background. He may be viewed by his autocratic superior with disdain, criticized for being vulgar or upstartish, or rejected for being weak and improper. To the detriment of efficiency and competence he may solicit ideas from anyone who happens to be in his vicinity at the time. Often his group meetings become too large to be effectively handled causing participation to be curtailed by many or monopolized by the more vociferous.

A major problem facing the democrat is that his equalitarian view may often achieve a leveling effect without his knowing it. The autocrat achieves leveling by attempting to eliminate individual differences and by enlarging the distance between him and his subordinates. But this form of leveling is basically intentional and fully predictable. Under democratic auspices, each man has a right to speak his ideas and be given consideration. Regardless of competence, ideas are often promoted by individuals who are exceptionally articulate or who have a great need to be heard. Bright ideas may get lost in the shuffle or often may not be given in a group atmosphere. Fugitive devices may be established whereby people with bright ideas can express themselves privately to the executive.

More important, the democrat's administrative group may become so attractive that the prestige and satisfaction of membership in it prevents many from making critical and disturbing remarks. Then, too, his unwillingness to tolerate conflict and his tendency to be congenial and pleasant may prevent roughhousing of ideas and opinions. When people need to be unpleasant or critical to him, his congeniality may restrain them. Leveling then results with sometimes tragic administrative consequences.

The democratic executive must constantly guard against leveling. It is a mistake to believe that conformity and inhibition occur solely under the autocrat. People conform for many reasons besides the fear of threat or the need to submit. They may practice leveling and conformity because the climate is simply too pleasant. To do otherwise would be ungentlemanly and improper and would meet severe criticism from others.

This is so great a problem that the democrat must master it or fail as an administrator. He can do this by anticipating leveling and assuming a critical attitude about himself and others.

His equalitarian attitude allows him to be critical without a show of emotional immaturity. He can express criticism and resentment openly without breaching his faith in human potentiality or destroying his congenial effect. It is precisely because he has successfully established a warm friendly climate that he can be openly critical without becoming personally antagonistic. This opportunity must be capitalized upon to offset the possible effects of leveling.

Freedom

The sharing orientation allows the subordinate to develop in directions most appropriate for him. The act of sharing is essential to preserving the individual's freedom. Freedom is one of the most difficult concepts to deal with in administration.

The autocrat, at times, partially withdraws obstacles and restraints in order to allow a little freedom. However, he only increases the anxiety of all concerned if they are not able to use their freedom productively. It is a mistake to believe that freedom is merely a condition of the situation. When the autocrat lets up on the reins, the individual may still feel oppressed because of the expectation that the reins will be pulled in again. One can hardly feel free if his freedom is not certain.

On the other hand, all freedom is conditional. It is subject to restraint and to proper use. Freedom requires a special kind of commitment from its pursuer. The commitment is like an act of faith, the faith that what is inherently good is practical. What is good may not be automatically practiced, but it is possible. Many administrators are not able to make this commitment. First, they often complain that the purposeful administration of freedom is dangerous and apt to boomerang; there are too many who will misuse and abuse freedom. Ad-

ministrators often say, "It is best to make no issue of freedom," "Silently release and restrain as the administrative needs
dictate," "Never fool with freedom for the sake of freedom."
In these arguments it is obvious that they cannot see freedom
as desirable in itself, or as an atmosphere that permits the
realization of other forms of good, or as something that es-
capes from one's clutches if not diligently pursued.

A genuine climate of freedom is not developed as a by-
product. No principle can be known for itself except in the
context of freedom. For example, power cannot be understood
apart from the opportunity to achieve power. To take freedom
as the first principle is to allow the recognition of what constitutes the lack of freedom. As long as the administrator does
not acknowledge the primacy of freedom as a principle, he will
not be aware of what degree of freedom is obtainable or already obtained. Nor will he aggressively pursue the cause of
freedom in general. While many businessmen become quite
concerned about the growing restrictions on their freedom,
they seldom become zealous about improving the condition of
freedom in their communities. Why do the clergy, lawyers, and
professors, not the businessmen, usually carry on the fight for
civil liberties, academic freedom, minority rights? The reason
is that businessmen typically are unaware that all freedoms
are interrelated. An attack on freedom in one area impinges
upon freedom in all other areas. Businessmen regard freedom
as by-products of the economic foundation, but free enterprise
does not guarantee all other freedoms. All freedoms must be
championed by those who wish to uphold their own.

Furthermore, the character of freedom as a by-product is
different from the character of freedom as a basic ideal. For
example, the individual who uses his life to achieve power
often claims to have achieved independence. However, close

scrutiny will show that the pursuit of power inevitably brings restraints. The responsibility to the self of protecting the power accumulated becomes restrictive in itself. He is free in the sense that he has a capacity to be selfishly responsible. But because he needs others to maintain his power, he is not free. He is very much dependent upon them, if not enslaved by them.

When freedom is accepted as a first principle of administration, it brings responsibility for the freedom of others and prohibits accumulation of power for self-defined ends. Freedom releases and develops others rather than restricting and using them.

The argument against the adoption of freedom as a first principle reflects lack of faith that freedom can become administratively practical. There is indeed a condition of risk operating. Freedom is another name for ambiguity. For that matter, the whole democratic method is filled with ambiguity. By its very nature it cannot root out dissenting elements such as autocracy or bureaucracy. It does not exist without diversity. Executives who shy away from a direct acknowledgment and acceptance of the democratic style are perhaps unable to tolerate ambiguity. They avoid that which they cannot tolerate. Their lack of faith in democracy is rooted in the incapacity to share themselves with others.

Some of the early subscribers to the democratic theme showed an amazing capacity to tolerate highly ambiguous situations brought on by conflicting opinion and views among different levels of authority. For example, when Pierre S. du Pont took over the presidency of General Motors in 1920 he adhered to the autocratic view. He strongly supported Kettering's plan for a copper-cooled engine against the protests of the engineers. He felt that the sale of the car with this engine might save General Motors from bankruptcy and preserve the huge investment of the du Pont funds. The engineers were overruled but their protests did gain expression by their direct control of the cars which were to be pushed when inventories were worked down enough. It turned out that the copper-cooled engine was not as well received as expected and from this experience du Pont learned a lesson. Ernest Dale points out that never again did he force a major investment of policy change over factual opposition. He became an avid subscriber to freedom of discussion. He used the board meetings, and especially the board committees, to inform the directors of changes contemplated and the reasons why, and invited their views and opinion. And to ensure against rubber stamping, he chose as directors men who could afford to be independent, either because of independent wealth or because of public prestige.[4]

When the executive goes this far to guarantee freedom of discussion, it seems clear that he feels certain about his ability to share his views with others. Confidence in one's capacity is displayed in the willingness to provide every opportunity for dissenting opinions. Alfred Sloan, whose concept of organization was adopted by du Pont as the basis for reconstructing General Motors, used many devices to make sure that everyone felt free to discuss. He would listen and ask searching questions before expressing his own view. "He might well take a subordinate's side against a superior in order to learn the former's real opinion."[5]

The capacity to share views and ideas is most ideally represented in the willingness to be overruled by men of inferior authority. "Sloan might sit and argue for hours. Then he

[4] Ernest Dale, *The Great Organizers*, McGraw-Hill, 1960, pp. 244–246.
[5] *Ibid.*, p. 246.

would sit back and say: 'Maybe I am wrong and we shouldn't do as I think.' And he would bear no grudge subsequently even though his opinion did not prevail."[6] The ability to avoid dogmatism when crucial facts have been overlooked shows profound faith in the administrative virtues of democracy. These pioneers of administrative democracy must have had a great capacity to share themselves with others. And this capacity stemmed from their faith in the administrative feasibility of democracy and their commitment to this view.

An atmosphere of informality often accompanies administrative freedom. The executive's gestures and mannerisms are spontaneous but relevant. He relies little upon conventional modes of dress to affect his proper relationships to people and has few inhibitions about the way people approach him. Titles, office, and status symbols are not essential to him although he is aware of how others might be in greater need of them. At times his behavior borders on the unconventional, although he is not preoccupied with this manner of behavior. Probably as good example as any is George Woods, chairman of First Boston Corporation, who practices persuasion with a gentle touch. Although nothing is quite as solemn as investment banking, he walks, sits, talks, tilts his hat, and has a style that is disarmingly casual. When he is dealing with a distinguished visitor, Woods will plop down into one of the overstuffed armchairs with his neck resting on the back rim and sometimes put his feet up on the table.[7] With the increase in the trend toward democracy in business, there has been a commensurate increase in informality. Company manners are no longer held sacred. Increasingly the executive can be himself. He can

[6] *Ibid.*, p. 246.
[7] Robert Sheehan, "First Man of First Boston," *Fortune*, June, 1959, pp. 144–167.

dress and behave as he pleases as long as it does not invite comment.

In democracy organizational formality is typically kept to the minimum of administrative necessity. The executive's problem may be the lack of orderliness. He may have a somewhat confused view of what is going on. With a tendency to interact a great deal with specific people, he may not be cognizant of their lack of integrated effort. He does not categorize and tends to repress whatever negative impressions he has of people so as to allow a new discovery of them in succeeding instances of interaction.

This lack of orderliness may place the subordinate on his own before he is actually ready. The executive's administrative connection to subordinates is spontaneous to the point of impulsiveness, allowing them opportunity to approach him on any subject at any time. If he is not careful, he can be easily "conned" and often his sensitivity is played upon to the detriment and impatience of others.

The absence of formal instructions places a premium upon initiative. It is largely up to the individual to find ways to show his ability. The superior effort that comes from the subordinate's identification with his real self is highly valued. The autocrat may grant freedom to ability that is placed in the service of the organization. But he remains the active judge of what needs to be done on behalf of the organization. The democrat wishes to allow his subordinates to participate in determining what needs to be done. To be free is to determine what one does rather than being given instructions. Therefore the executive endeavors to develop his subordinates and make their actions largely their own. Crawford Greenewalt puts it this way. "Contributions to the joint effort will vary in kind as they vary in importance. Some will contribute in brilliant flashes of form; others through their steadiness, persistence, or the grueling and often overlooked grind of hard routine work. The important thing to the organization is that each individual be given the opportunity to exploit his talents to the fullest, in the way best suited to his personality."[8]

The subordinate's actions must be controlled to some extent to be sure they show a responsibility to the welfare of the organization and are integrated with the activities of others. The democratic executive who has succeeded and advanced to the top management has a trained or artificially contrived reluctance to allow opportunity of self-expression in crucial areas without some assurance of responsible results. Contrary to what many people believe about the democrat, he is not disposed to delegate freely but rather responsibly.

So that the subordinate may develop the ability and power to initiate his own acts, alternate courses of action must be made available to him whenever he shows tendencies against his and the organization's welfare. Then, through his own choice he will be able to select modes of behavior that are more proper and beneficial. Freedom of choice is an important human need, but it is a freedom that can safely be given only to individuals who are well informed about all the possible alternatives and their consequences. Helping a subordinate arrive at the decision that the superior thinks is best requires careful communication. Of course, the democrat's character traits allow him to interact freely and effectively in giving information, posing alternatives, and suggesting possible consequences. He communicates effectively with his subordinates, keeping them informed about all aspects of problems being considered.

The autocrat communicates by taking the role of the source

[8] Crawford Greenewalt, *The Uncommon Man,* McGraw-Hill, 1959, p. 47.

of information with his subordinates as receivers. This over-simplified communication system creates major difficulties because it does not admit that error might be found at the source. If communication is bad, it is assumed that there is something wrong with the receivers. Consequently, the subordinate must rely completely on himself to keep up with what is going on. In other words, the autocrat substitutes authority for good communication.

The democrat assumes the responsibility for keeping people informed. If misunderstandings arise, it is because he has failed to convey to others the proper meanings. Unlike the autocrat, who believes that communication is simply the passing of words from one person to another, the democrat realizes that words may have different meanings for different people. Consequently, he relies upon a free and open conversational technique, allowing differences of interpretation to arise in order to prevent misunderstanding later.

The autocrat's attitude toward error is similar to his attitude toward communication. Naturally all executives want as few errors as possible, but the autocrat approaches the problem through his authority. He passes an order against errors and feels that he has dealt with the problem. If an error is made, it must be due to the subordinate's incompetence or loose moral character. The fault never lies at the source.

The democrat realizes that mistakes cannot be dealt with by force and discipline. Both superior and subordinate are subject to error, and force may only increase anxiety to the point where mistakes are aggravated. Increased communication and constructive criticism will be much more effective. Even if major errors are committed which might prove threatening to his administrative career, the democrat tries to avoid showing vindictiveness. He may move the subordinate into a position which will not be as crucial to his and the organization's continued welfare, but not unless he is sure that the error was intentional or indicative of a general tendency to treat major problems too lightly. In his ideal administrative format, a man can make a mistake without undue anxiety, the first time at least.

We have been discussing the type of freedom the democrat tries to develop in his organization—freedom of discussion, absence of formality, encouragement of initiative, freedom of choice, and the like. But the absence of restrictive influences in an administrative format is only a situation which must be used by the subordinate. He must have the desire and ability to act productively within this situation. The democrat is always aware of a tendency to misuse and abuse this opportunity, and therefore, by means of his constant interaction with them, he attempts to establish firm guidelines for the responsible channeling of activity. He keeps a careful, but friendly, eye on all activities.

Because he is not suspicious and distrustful, his subordinates may seem to get by with pretenses of responsible use of their freedom of action. But, because he tends to restrain overt acts of aggression, he may know more than they think he does. It is characteristic of a democratic administrator to have many of these "secrets." More is known than is said. To offend is worse than to reveal, and truth is less important than harmony. Conflict is allowed to occur if it is polite, rational, and administratively helpful, but even then conflict scares the democrat, especially about matters that might reflect on honesty or injure pride and dignity. In many instances matters are not rectified because of his reluctance to bring up a difficult issue.

The tendency to avoid offending often means inhibiting

negative reactions in general. The democrat may therefore be unable to channel his aggressions effectively; he often lacks follow-through and the "killer's instinct." He should fire more people and discipline more than he does. But the organization is amazingly free of parochial viewpoints and personal backbiting. He does not tolerate confidences that are manipulative devices nor does he allow himself to be used by a weak individual who needs a wailing wall. With these reservations, he is apt to help the subordinate use his freedom by making the resources of the organization available to him. His organization is in this respect open. He is most apt to distribute resources and opportunties according to need. Herein lies an essential ingredient of his executive style that is distinct from the autocrat and bureaucrat.

The autocrat's inability to meet people on their own terms prevents him from distributing the resources at his disposal along the lines of the needs of his subordinates. He releases these resources upon them to the minimum of administrative necessity. His approach is closed, restrictive, and overcontrolled.

The democrat is supportive rather than restrictive. He is there to help them do what normally they could not do by themselves. He casts himself in the role of a servant and aid. His personal needs are not actively involved in his interpretation of their needs. In every way he will do as much for them as is possible, including giving them financial support.

Both the autocrat and bureaucrat tend to use money as a control device. The bureaucrat is particularly interested in using budgets as control devices. So sacred are budgets that living within the budget becomes the major goal rather than using the budget to achieve the most effective allocation of funds. Money is not the democrat's chief tool of motivation and control. His character allows him to motivate through identifying and interacting with people with guidance and general helpfulness.

But more importantly, he motivates and controls through the assignment of new opportunities and responsibilities. Jobs with prestige go to those who at certain times need ego boosting, challenging jobs to those who begin to suffer boredom, and routine assignments to those who have been long on the firing line and need a break. His administrative format is flexible to accommodate the need satisfactions of his subordinates. When it is used with a clear understanding of their emotional states and with their full support and appreciation, he achieves a control not commonly found in the other executive styles. His last resort is the use of finance and gratuities of his office for the purpose of achieving control. As a result he gives opportunity for subordinates to develop their ability. Ideally they are both free from many of the usual administrative restrictions and free to develop their abilities and opportunities.

A flexible and open administration does not mean an absence of control. Democracy and laissez faire are inimical. When freedom is valued, it is valued for all, and to work toward this end requires imposing rather severe responsibilities on superiors and subordinates alike. This means that the individual is not allowed to shift for himself nor is he allowed to remain indifferent while others are in need of help. Nor does it mean that the aggressive individuals are allowed to pursue ambitions contrary to their own or others' better interests.

This latter point is a delicate subject. If an individual is superior in mind or temperament, should he not be given opportunity to express himself? The question drives to the heart of democracy. Superiority must be given a chance to make its contribution. But not in a manner potentially threatening to democracy itself. One who has a stronger impulse to power should not be allowed to express it except in ways that add to the common good. Democracy is not out to help bad boys to be bad, but rather to help them become productive for the benefit of all. Many have strong impulses to dominate others. The real test of the democratic executive is how well can he help to give them release in sublimated forms. In fact, this is the central problem of administration.

In an autocratic administration a person with a strong power impulse can find release for his hostile tendencies in the hierarchical orientation. However, in a democratic administration he is not free to institute a mechanism of behavior that perverts the essential character of the administrative style. If he generalizes his hierarchical orientation into a power orientation, he may still be upset over insufficient opportunity to practice his bicycle psychology. The executive should not be free to be submissive any more than he should be free to be domineering. Both are inimical to the ideals of democracy.

The democrat has a real problem with autocrats. They are inclined to consider him weak and to reject his administrative premises or take advantage of them. To defend himself against being used by autocrats, the democrat will restrict their opportunity to influence and control. At the same time, he will attempt to engage their power impulses productively by establishing extra high standards of performance and achievement. He thereby keeps them busy and appeals to their sense of mastery.

Rationality

The autocrat likes no one near him or his throne. He is not psychologically prepared to share himself with others. His inability to believe in human potentiality prevents participa-

tion or holds it to a minimum. But basically he does not believe in the rationality of people in general. They are basically
stupid and lazy and will never be much of anything without
the few who are capable of seeing reality and ordering conditions for them.

An implication of this view is that man obeys no law save
that of power. Man responds to the threat of force or deprivation rather than love and understanding. In other words, man
is basically antisocial but becomes social only to serve his own
interests. The mechanism operating is prudence, which is the
fusion of fear and reason. He becomes productively antisocial
or intelligently selfish. Reason obeys best the dictates of power
and authority.

The autocratic view presents the individual and the organization as antithetical but not irreconcilable. The individual must learn to make intelligent use of organization or be
used by it for ends other than his own. Reconciliation may
occur through domination or submission. In the first case he
masters the organization to the extent that he determines what
others are to do. Participation is inimical to his concept of
control. He controls by minimizing human interaction.

In the past this restriction went as far as to exclude social
discourse and such personal habits as smoking. Any spontaneity except that which was directed toward the superior's
interests was considered improper. With the growth of the
bureaucratic theme spontaneity became viewed as inefficient.
In both cases the human impulses were to be regimented because they were basically hostile and self-centered.

Such a view of man may be a projection of the autocrat's
own hostilities. For example, Thomas Hobbes, the great
theorist of autocracy, was himself an autocrat who ruled his
household tyrannically. Freud, who also believed that man

was good insofar as external force made him good, tended to accept the hierarchy of human differences. Apparently he viewed differences among people as relations of superiority and subordination. In his own life pattern he tended to worship authority and look down his nose on weakness. This is evidenced by his impatience with servants, in his rudeness with women at times. With maids and cab drivers he appeared to be exploitive and even mean. He spat on the stairs to annoy a particularly neat housekeeper. Apparently he had all of the traits of a nineteenth-century bourgeois gentleman who typically had little respect for the lower classes. His technique was itself autocratic. The patient was placed on a couch in a passive, reclining position with the analyst in back of him so as not to see him and to avoid interaction. Free association did not permit a genuine two-way encounter but rather encouraged a kind of shadow boxing with the doctor and patient taking their turns at being boxer and shadow.

In contrast, the democrat assumes potential good and a high degree of rationality in people. To him knowledge and freedom are interdependent. The health of an organization is measured by the awareness that people have of what is going on. Given the necessary information and training, people will make wise choices and accept rational decisions made on their behalf. People are at base socially responsible. The democrat must believe that the individual and organization are mutually supportive and stimulating. Without this faith in the potential supremacy of reason over the irrational drives, the executive will not be able to relax his control to the point of encouraging genuine democracy. President Greenewalt of du Pont has said the same thing in different words, "It is only human to think highly of one's own method, and it calls for Christian tolerance to reach the understanding required to endorse methods and approaches which are not one's own."[9]

Among many executives today there is a kind of jostling and sparring that appears to result from respect and appreciation for differences of opinion. Closer examination shows that it is not genuine regard for the other person, but rather hostility at work, and what appears to be a free exchange of ideas is really shadow boxing for the sake of excelling in administrative upmanship.

In practice the democrat develops for the members of his organization a structural framework for achieving productive activity and experiences that serve to unite them in common endeavor. Structure is used to facilitate rather than restrict. Within the structure freedom is maximized. This is what President Greenewalt meant when he said that individuality must not be allowed to run rampant over organizational purposes. The structure may be constant, but its function is made up of hundreds of separate tasks. It is the accomplishment of the separate task rather than the particular technique used to approach them that should jibe with the structure. "Responsibility, authority, and the right to use individual methods must go hand in hand." Hence, the structure of authority must lead to loyalty to the tasks at hand and freedom to perform them as one thinks best. The opportunity to choose one's method is essential to democracy.

The Use of the Group

The administrative use of the concept of rationality is also found in the belief that better decisions are made through interaction. In other words, the products of interaction may reflect the workings of superior reason. Thus, the basic vehicle for the implementation of the rational theme is the adminis-

[9] *Ibid.*, p. 12.

trative group. Invariably the democratic executive is committed to majority opinion and only when his administrative
group is incapable of making a decision will he make one for
them, especially in matters of policy.

Many maintain that decision-making is less valid and more
hazardous when left to the group. They maintain that there
is no essential incompatibility between the spirit of democracy
and one-man decisions about a problem which has been freely
discussed by all members with interests involved. To be sure,
there are many ways to develop the concept of administrative
democracy. But often this argument is based on an inability to
assume personal responsibility while dispersing power and
authority.

There is no essential reason why the executive's administrative group cannot be used authoritatively if the executive is
willing to assume responsibility for its acts and decisions. After
all, the real question is not who is responsible, but how to
make the best decisions. As a matter of faith the democrat is
committed to developing a group competent to rely on for
making decisions. Not just any group is capable of achieving a
higher degree of reason than the individual alone might provide. The executive works at building thoroughly competent
men who are able to interact in such a way that a truly more
productive decision comes forth than would have been made
by an individual alone.

Many executives lack the ability to develop a group that is
more competent collectively than the individuals are sep-
arately. Then, too, there are many administrative situations in
which the group inherited by the top executive is not easily
shaped into a democratic team. The Pentagon is a case in
point. The chiefs of each of the three services are typically

strong-willed men, often more interested in advancing their departmental objectives than the total defense effort. Few secretaries have made productive use of their collective judgments or conflicting opinions. Former Secretary of Defense Thomas S. Gates followed the simple but novel technique of joining the meetings of the Joint Chiefs of Staff whenever matters on which they disagreed were under discussion. By this method he became known as the most decisive secretary because he could iron out disagreement and help arrive at decisions acceptable to the Joint Chiefs of Staff. Other secretaries had to make decisions in the dark about controversial matters.

In some cases the democrat will be responsive to the dissenting opinion of one group member to the extent that he will consider his action a veto. However, the trend seems to favor curtailment of veto-like opinions if a coherent view would be sacrificed. Senator Henry Jackson has recently issued a report on the overhaul of the State Department. He stated, "The possible suppression of opposing views by a strong chairman is far less dangerous than the disappearance of any coherent view at all into a quicksand of generalities under the rule of liberum veto [veto exercised by a single member]." Such an attitude is not uncommon and is most likely to be found where committees are quite numerous and chairmen need to be encouraged to be strong and vigorous.

The democrat's administrative group is not necessarily a constant entity. The democrat may use small groups that afford greater possibility of offering good ideas and rejecting wrong ones. Larger groups may be used when the problem appears to need more than immediate formation of opinion. But in either case, groups may be used for purposes of arriving at valid decisions and also getting those decisions accepted. However, the larger the group the more likely that the group judgment has more power over the individual members.

Large groups generally produce a greater variety of hypotheses and apparently a greater number of checks against errant hypotheses, but at the same time they are apt to create more of a tendency for suggestions to converge or to be "leveled." To some extent both tendencies represent healthy reactions in groups. But they also tend to work against each other. Control is important here in that the executive must aid the group in keeping its "mind" open as long as possible so as to provide the greatest number of hypotheses at the earliest point in the group process, then help the group to close its "mind" when it appears that enough hypotheses have been developed and a decision must be sought.

Needless to say, the skill of developing the forces of the group is of such a high level that only a few are able to effect this result. For this reason the democrat's committees are more apt to be small in order to arrive at a difficult decision and large in order to arrive at a consensus based upon the immediate formation of opinion. Often the two are combined, a small group works out the decision which is then presented to the larger group, where the forces of group cohesiveness are better able to help enforce the small group judgment.

Because the democrat is committed to the inherent rationality of man, he will base his arguments on rational systems of thought. He will avoid romantic, philosophical, and slanted word choices. Although he does try to avoid using loaded words and fallacious arguments to make his points, he does attempt to use social ideas based upon practical experiences to win others to his way of thinking. And he is prepared to accept counterarguments of the same nature. One example of how this technique may be expressed was the administrative be-havior of Secretary of State Herter. His predecessor, Dulles, was a strong, forceful personality with a fanatical zeal in what he believed. He attempted to browbeat others into submission to his own views. Herter let the facts of power speak for them-selves. He seemed to know better how arguments and crises would evolve and a calm, thoughtful climate characterized his orderly pursuit of winning friends and opponents. Herter was moved more easily by the persuasive arguments of others and in the end derived more prestige and respect from the Allies than Dulles who could not stand to be converted.

The democrat's task is essentially to provide the conditions whereby his subordinates can actively participate in shaping the direction and character of their mode of life. Anyone who is aware of community problems knows that one of the most difficult tasks is to get people to participate in the affairs that so intimately tie them together as an organization. Once they are together, the next step is to help them to make wise and considerate use of each other in formulating their specific goals and determining the most efficient means. In other words, getting individuals to function as a cohesive group is not easy—not because they are inherently irrational or hostile, but because often they are indifferent or poorly equipped. To transform a collection of individuals into a compact unit with singularity of purpose and harmony of means is no small feat.

Cohesiveness represents the total pressures acting on mem-bers to remain in the group. In other words, cohesiveness results from the attraction of the group for its members. From cohesiveness stems the "internal power of the group," that is, the group's power to induce change in its members. The de-gree of power inherent in the group is in direct proportion to the force on the member to remain in the group. There are fewer deviates in highly cohesive groups than in less cohesive groups.

But there are several kinds of cohesiveness. It can be based on personal attraction and group prestige, on the performance of a task, or on the members' needs to be part of a group. The democratic executive avoids cohesiveness based on personal attraction, because too often the group members may want to transform discussion into pleasant conversation. If cohesiveness is based on group prestige, members will not risk endangering their status—they act cautiously, concentrate on their own actions, and adjust readily to others' viewpoints. When cohesiveness is based on the performance of a task, group members want to complete the activity as quickly and efficiently as possible. They are useful to each other when they can use their time efficiently.

If the democrat achieves only minimum cohesiveness, he must deal with people acting independently of each other and with little consideration for each other. They do not try to adjust to the other members and each member is concerned only with his own discussion. The democrat must take care in controlling the flow of communication to avoid conflicts that upset the orderly pursuit of accomplishing the task before them.

Group cohesiveness may be mixed and erratic. For example, members may be attracted to a group for many different reasons—some may join for task accomplishment, some for personal satisfaction, others for group prestige, and still others for a mixture of all three. The executive must relate to the members in terms of their particular attraction to his group. But he must use his relationship to build group cohesiveness around the advantages membership in the group provides each member in carrying out his responsibilities. The standard of the group is the administrative responsibility to each other as colleagues.

A strong cohesive group, a "team," is what the democrat needs to make his administrative format workable. Because of the disadvantages of leveling and inefficiency, he must master the group. And because of the advantages he must serve the group. He must control and serve.

The group cannot be viewed as a democratic resource in itself. How the group is used is important, but more important are the motives for which the group is used. Around any given conference table today in business or government there sit many autocrats who have adopted the group as a means for making the climb up the ladder to higher positions of power.

The group may do for the autocrat what the system does for the bureaucrat. It may provide a means of rendering hostile feelings productive and useful. Or he may come to use the group as a way to assert his impulsiveness. In either case, the group may become a convenient way to dominate or submit. There is nothing inherent in the group that is not inherent in the individual. If the autocrat can dominate individuals, he can dominate groups of individuals as well. The setting for the act is not as important as the motive of the act itself.

The domination of a group cannot always be detected for what it is. Autocrats may conform to group pressure because the act of conforming is itself a way to influence and control. Or the autocrat may agree with norms and decisions to keep from being genuinely influenced by them. Since he does not really believe in them, he can pervert their true aims to achieve his own purposes.

The need to broaden the basis of participation in order to administer massive complex organizations effectively brought forth the group. It has the trappings of democracy, but it may merely represent a different form of sublimation of the autocratic impulses. While the genuine democrat performs the function of releasing and directing the affiliative impulses, the autocrat may use the opportunity to gain power. The executive may find it necessary to use power in serving the goals of collective achievement and unity. If he is committed to democratic ideals, he will keep impulses of power and order from perverting the aims of productive unity and cohesiveness. If he is not firm in his commitment to democracy, he may exploit and abuse the opportunity to use power or ensuing consequences. If he does not trust his own power impulses, he may severely restrain the power drives in others. If he cannot respect the power needs of others, he may effect his and their usefulness.

But the autocrat is not the only one sitting at the democrat's conference table today. There is also the bureaucrat and he is sometimes as difficult to identify as the autocrat. A growing number of executives today cling first and foremost to the bureaucratic style, because it represents the safe, cautious, and certain approach to executive problems. Naturally, whatever they adopt from the democratic style is pressed into the bureaucratic mold.

Rather than use the group to broaden the base of participation, the bureaucrat uses the group to overcome the unreliability of the individual. As such the group becomes an appendage of the system to be used to help internalize in each individual the needs and demands of the system. Discussion is not aimed at achieving spontaneity, but rather to enhance the adoption of rules and regulations, procedures and policies, and the sentiments of the bureaucracy. The administrative group, whether it is a committee or board, may acquire a systematic quality that may snuff out freedom just as surely as autocratic rule.

Bureaucracy vs. Democracy

If allowed to act without restraint, autocratic executives would quickly build up a number of power camps, each seeking to overcome the other. The consequences would be the break-up of large organizational systems into many small units, each led by an autocrat seeking to become free of the others. Rather than risk this break-up, modern organizations prefer rigidity, even at the danger of slow death through structural stagnation.

The high degree of permanency and continuity of today's massive organization is largely due to the ability of executives to direct their energies into systematically rationalized and specialized channels. The integrated and controlled nature of large-scale business and government curtails the possibility of the drastic changes which appeal to the autocrat. Autocratic impulses must be well restricted to small-scale changes and effects. Threats and obstacles emerge only within the confines of small programs, each of which belongs to a total pattern. The over-all pattern is changed only by limited variations within limited areas. Changes are gradual and impersonal rather than direct and personal.

In effect, bureaucracy is rapidly engulfing the autocrat. Autocracy is no longer the prominent enemy of democracy. For many executives, the bureaucratic is the basic style into which elements from the autocratic and democratic styles are incorporated. The autocratic base is becoming obsolete.

If the swing from autocracy to bureaucracy is as general as it seems, it means that for many the system, not the individual or group, is the basis of administration. Skill rather than energy, thought rather than action, precision rather than decisiveness, reliability rather than courage, efficiency rather than productivity, rules rather than commands, all represent this swing from autocracy to bureaucracy. Thus, the denunciation of the autocratic executive by enthusiasts of democracy may be based upon a mistaken notion of who their real opponent is. It may not be personal autocracy as much as the subtle, silent, anonymous autocracy of the system. It is rules ruling rather than the self ruling.

As the executive becomes more bureaucratic freedom will be found not in the ability to develop oneself, but in the ability to develop the system. Equality of opportunity and dignity will become rationalized into scales of meritorious achievement and performance.

When the bureaucrat shares, he shares precisely. He loves order and he loves in an orderly manner. His affiliative impulses are modified by his rigid character, precise training, and infallible expertese. When he shares his competency, he shares it with the office and not the individual, with the role and not the person. He needs others merely for their functional roles in the system. When he shares he expects return in kind. Since he does not share himself, his thoughts and feelings that cannot be returned or systematized, he expects no one to share his personal thoughts and feelings with him.

Those who feel that the bureaucrat has eliminated the autocrat also fail to discern the true problem. The bureaucrat and autocrat are at base the same. They both represent power, the one systematic and the other personal, respectively. The real struggle is not between the power of order and love of power, but rather between the loving of order and the ordering of love.

It is a struggle between restricting the human impulses, binding them into highly integrated and rationalized systems of beliefs and functions, and releasing the human impulses, giving them freedom to achieve their own form of productive expression.

With order as the primary executive style, love or service becomes compulsive. The problem of how, when, and whom to help becomes based not on need, but on duty. Armed with the book the executive follows the rules or passes the buck. He is properly efficient and correct, and moral and sentimental consequences are left to others.

The democratic enthusiasts must press the attack or suffer the consequences of growing bureaucracy. The struggle between autocracy, bureaucracy, and democracy must not be resolved into what may amount to a bureaucratic solution. Neither the instrumental nor systematic use of democratic values is the answer to today's problem of administration. The danger is seen in the younger executives who believe that administration consists largely of a battery of technical experts presided over by a human relations expert.

As many executives whose emotional impulses are anchored in democracy must be developed as there are executives today seemingly anchored in bureaucracy. The emergence of the bureaucrat may represent a needed addition to a society growing beyond manageable proportions. However, he should not represent the final stage of executive development. Autocracy and bureaucracy must not become the disproportionate result of size and complexity.

If the democratic style fails to achieve the necessary respect and prestige to press power and order into the service of human freedom and dignity, the present executive amalgam will not represent a decided improvement over the power-driven executive of the past. It does not seem possible that the executive's emerging sense of social responsibility can be sustained without a rather extensive adoption within his organization of the democratic style of administratioin. Without strong faith in the administrative feasibility of democracy, the executive cannot be expected to attempt to use the instruments of power and order to serve the human needs of society.

Sharing his skills, abilities, and knowledge by intense activity in his society and broadening the base of participation within his organization are indeed substantial beginnings in the direction of a democratic style. Just as love is capable of modifying the hate impulses in the individual, so democracy is capable of bringing the executive's instruments of power and order within the range of genuine social and moral responsibility. However, as long as bureaucracy is the major anchorage, the executive will wield power and share his skills because of duty and the necessity of preserving himself and the organization rather than because of a genuine feeling for his fellowman.

The Combination of Styles

The argument is often heard that democracy in business is at best an instrument to be pressed into service of authority and efficiency. The argument is based on the false notion that democracy must be accepted either in a pure form or in the context of the other two. In the latter case it cannot really be democracy.

There is no democracy in the absence of some degree of autocracy and bureaucracy. Freedom does not just happen—people must organize to achieve it. Freedom is always related to the power of the individuals to act and to instruments chosen for transforming power into efficient action. The pursuit of happiness and abundance depends upon the efficiency with which power and other means are used to serve communal needs. Hence, freedom is dependent upon systems of action and upon respect for power and authority necessary to establish and maintain them.

It is much the same with regard to power, order, and love, the basic tap roots of the three executive styles of autocracy, bureaucracy, and democracy. Powerless love and loveless power strike offsetting blows to human progress and happiness. Similarly, disorderly love and loveless order are equally barren of producing human achievement. Total weakness and inability to act decisively and vigorously, inefficiency in administrative aim and performance are incompatible with the act of sharing. One is not free to share unless he has something that is worth sharing. He is at best only free to withdraw and to fail. A perfect state of administration with love the unconditional victor is an impossible condition. Love, order, and power cannot be defined nor productively expressed without each other.

Therefore, the idea is absurd that the ultimate administrative format needed to run business and government is unblemished democracy. The question is not how powerful or efficient is business or government, but rather how capable and willing are executives to place power and efficiency in the service of those values that lie central to democracy. How capable and willing are executives to provide activities of organized behavior that follow human choice and dignity?

All claims by the executive that he is assuming his social and moral responsibilities are idle and unproductive unless his actions are translated into well-implemented and well-organized behavior. He must be autocratic and bureaucratic. But equally barren are his claims if work and the products of work are imposed upon men capable of making choices and participating in their implementation. He must also be democratic. The practices of autocracy and bureaucracy conflict with democracy when they inhibit the purpose of democracy. When they do not they are legitimate techniques of administration. Such is the executive view that is firmly based in democracy.

CHAPTER 8

THE NEUROCRAT AND
THE FLEXIBLE EXECUTIVE

The executive occupies a central position in which he must constantly choose between alternatives, make decisions, and reformulate them. The intense pressures that bombard him may develop and heighten profound feelings of anxiety. These feelings of apprehension and uncertainty may come and go so infrequently that the executive may not attribute any importance to them. Or he may be aware of having depressions or feelings of inadequacy without realizing how they are related to his role. For all practical purposes he appears to function productively according to the realistic objectives of his executive responsibility. The degree of anxiety acknowledged may not surpass the normal. However, the degree of anxiety is not always consciously known to the individual. The executive may have anxiety without knowing it and it, more than anything else, may determine the way he performs his role.

Escape from Administrative Anxiety

In the executive world there is much about which to be anxious. Let us briefly review the sources of anxiety which we discussed in Chapters 1, 2, and 3. As his activity has extended from the traditional base of operating within a specific organization to taking a responsible role within the many institutions of society, including politics, government, education, the community, the element of the unknown has been likewise increased. And as these other institutions, government and unions in particular, have stepped up the tempo of their taboos and pressures upon business, the executive has found more and more about which to become concerned.

Take, for example, the recent crackdown upon collusive practices in the electrical manufacturing industry. It is well known that for some time executives among the major manufacturers were price fixing. Of course, such activity is unlawful and was never explicitly approved by the companies. Yet, many of the executives sent to prison felt that their activities were given implicit sanction. One executive interviewed by the author went to great lengths to show that many of them were expected to perform in this manner as a condition of their job tenure. Even though they heard rumors that this activity was being investigated, they never thought it would be interpreted as it was. Overnight, with the change of administration in Washington, they were transformed from respectable executives into criminals. Approach any corporation official and he may speak for hours about the uncertainty of dealing with government. The many requirements and pressures from government are seldom carefully spelled out. There is much room for interpretation by both parties. And, hence, much room to be caught up in difficulty and error.

We have not yet discussed the risks involved in the market place. The consumer is fickle, quick to change without apparent rationality or predictability. And about as shifty is the competitor, who must anticipate and control the same fickle consumer.

In addition, the business executive is one of the most important members of our society because of the emphasis placed upon economic prosperity. Also, because everything is so organized in society, there is no way to escape from ego deprivation except by finding self-expression within organizations. The business executive, along with all other administrators, is now required to be our chief guardian of democracy. The executive role holds both unprecedented responsibility and uncertainty. Suffice it to say, few occupations are as vulnerable to the problem of anxiety as the executive's.

The executive may not be conscious of the pressures he feels because anxiety is painful and must be avoided. The source of anxiety may be repressed by many mechanisms of the mind. The basic method used to disguise the source of anxiety is rationalization. He attempts to give dignity and creditability to his feelings of helplessness and uncertainty. This method transforms the anxiety into an objective fear. Fear is a special condition of the emotions—it is a reaction to danger that is objectively verifiable by others. The individual's emotional feelings of uncertainty are justified. Also, he is relieved of responsibility for his difficulties. The fault is not his but some external factor beyond his control.

For example, if the executive is anxious about the future because he has just been fired, his reaction would no doubt be considered justifiable. If he is anxious about the future because he has just been given a promotion, his reaction would seem unreasonable, unless, of course, the organization typically promotes executives to sit on the shelf for the rest of their lives.

The attempt to rationalize anxiety includes finding specific, objective reasons for his feelings of doubt and uncertainty. The business executive may concentrate on specific acts of government, his superiors, authority-granting groups, or his subordinates, which he perceives as hostile, intractable, or unscrupulous. He may find and use any objective evidence needed to support his arguments. And what factual evidence is lacking will be supplied by his imagination. Thus, there are executives who picture the government as the villain about to destroy freedom of man. All blame for the restrictions on businessmen rests with irresponsible or naïve politicians. There is a struggle between freedom represented by free enterprise and tyranny represented by bureaucratic government. Or the whipping boy may be unreasonable labor unions or the fickle consumer public. These villains are presented in such a way that fear seems to be an entirely justifiable and rational reaction. He is, therefore, not responsible for his troubles. He never thinks that these villains might not be as bad as he says they are. He may not be aware that his fear does not originate from objective circumstance, but rather from inner feelings of insecurity.

The Comprehensive Solution

In order to cope with ambiguity and anxiety the executive may depend upon absolute and certain answers to his problems. The problems are clearly defined with solutions precisely spelled out to guarantee ultimate results. Thus, the answer to encroachment of government or unions upon the rights of business to freely conduct its affairs may be to oppose vigorously all efforts of government or unions. In the showdown that ensues the executive finds his greatest feelings of certainty and justification. Their acts of hostility prove what he has believed all along, namely, they are to be feared and opposed. Whether he loses or wins the struggle, the gain or loss is only temporary. There is just enough justification for his fears to keep the deep anxiety alive and well fed.

He becomes sure that what he is doing is right. The cause he serves is to him his condition of authority. On behalf of his mission he dominates his organization and the people therein. They all become to him the servants of his great mission of fighting against this or that evil represented by his real villains. The more the executive feels trapped in the intricate network of his fears and anxiety, the more he must cling to the delusion that he is right and perfect in everything and the more he must reject any direct or indirect insinuation that he may be wrong or need to change. He finds in his cause a comprehensive solution not only to a specific conflict, but to all conflicts that may accompany his performance of the executive role. Instead of seeing and accepting the necessity of changing something within himself or his organization, he can shift the responsibility to the outside world and thereby escape from his own difficulty. The anxiety is preserved under the auspices of a fearless, courageous dedication to an altruistic and noble cause.

Although the bureaucratic and democratic styles may serve as anchorages for his neurotic tendencies, his solution fits the autocratic style. His bicycle psychology is represented by subservience to his cause or mission and by domination of his organization and its authority-granting and interest groups. On behalf of free enterprise, union immorality, governmental tyranny, consumer needs and whims, he arbitrarily orders the necessary combination of human endeavor to surmount the obstacles and pressures. Whatever the realistic pressures and restraints may be, his central position prescribes that authority-granting groups above and subordinates below rely upon his interpretation. He becomes the sole effective force, an autocrat.

Although this autocrat may appear to be the complete master of every important situation, he is frightened and insecure. Of course, he may be conscious only of his power and success. His condition is described as neurotic.

Not all executives are neurotic. Many are not overwhelmed by the ambiguities of the executive role. To be sure, the real dangers and hazards inherent in the executive role are great. The ambiguities described in previous chapters are not the fictitious constructions of a detached mind. The healthy executive is aware of these risks and not afraid to accept them. The neurotic tends to distort them to accommodate his inner forces and needs. He may imagine them to be much greater, less, or different. He resorts to the escape mechanism of rationalization to avoid his feelings of anxiety.

The mature executive may very well believe that action must be taken in the direction that the neurotic prescribes. He may honestly feel that unions are getting out of hand, government is snuffing out freedom, consumers are responsible for collusive practices among competitors. He may achieve a position of power in his organization necessary to attack these conditions. But the mature executive does these things on a rational basis, the neurotic on a basis of irrational striving.

In this sense striving for power is not necessarily a neurotic symptom, just as the wish for order or love is certainly not in itself a neurotic trend. It is commonly believed that the difference between normal and neurotic striving for power is the extent to which it is born of feelings of strength or weakness. In a normal person the striving for power may develop from the realization of his own superior strength, whether it be physical strength or mental capacities. Or strivings for power may be the necessary means to attain a healthy, socially desirable goal or purpose.[1]

It is not a condition of health to inhibit or deny expression to one's unique qualities. The truly superior individual may find a way to express his advantage and in so doing achieve enormous power over others. To be timid or anxious in the use of this power and to inhibit or view it with disdain are symptoms of the lack of maturity.[2] Superior capacity is best revealed in accomplishments. If one is unable or fearful of employing his supposedly superior capacity, it is questionable as to whether he is actually superior. In short, one who is genuinely capable of influencing others more than they influence him is not necessarily neurotic.

For example, Churchill and Hitler have been pictured in Chapter 5 as similar in one major respect. They both achieved a quality of presence. Wherever they went they dominated to the point that others had little breathing space. Yet, one of them no doubt will be recorded by historians as neurotic.

No single man worked as hard as Churchill to prevent World War II. In contrast, no single man worked as hard as Hitler to bring on World War II. Oddly enough, as much as Churchill fought to prevent the war, in one sense he actually needed it. History would have recorded him as a political failure if it had not been for Hitler's war. When he became prime minister, he felt for the first time in his life that he had the opportunity to use all his genius and energy for a cause in which he passionately believed. He wrote, "In my long political experience I had held most of the great offices of State, but I readily admit that the post which had now fallen to me was the one I like best. Power, for the sake of lording

[1] See Karen Horney, *The Neurotic Personality of Our Time*, Norton, 1938.
[2] *Ibid.*

it over fellow creatures or adding to personal pomp, is rightly judged base. But power in a national crisis, when a man believes he knows what orders should be given, is a blessing."[3]

This motive for power is born of feelings of inner strength and becomes actively expressed in realistic objectives. Hitler is commonly believed to have sought out power because of strong inner feelings of weakness.. His passion for exclusive power and his hostility toward those who retained it were manifested early in his life. The craving to cut a grand figure prevented him from adjusting to reality as a boy and as a man forced him to create reality to conform to his inner needs. He made Germany over to fit his own personality. Hitler sought a comprehensive solution, which lay in destroying all obstacles to himself, first within Germany and thereafter within the whole world. Unlike the power drive of Churchill, Hitler's was out of contact with realistic objectives. He destroyed himself and Germany, whereas Churchill saved England and the cause of human decency.

Thus, the executive who dominates to the point of being autocratic may or may not operate from a base of healthy motives. Few observers have ascribed neurotic tendencies to Churchill, and yet he used his wartime powers to a greater extent than Roosevelt, who has often been described as neurotic. It is all too easy to impute unhealthy motives to those who enjoy the exercise of power. Why should the calisthenics of power be any more harmful to the personality than the calisthenics of order or love? Excessive dependence on the approval or affection of others or on tidiness and systematic routine is a neurotic activity as much as excessive dependence on the need to dominate others.

[3] Virginia Cowles, Winston Churchill, the Era and the Man, Grosset & Dunlap, 1940, p. 324.

The manifest picture of modern life in western society clearly indicates that economic, political, social, and moral purposes are all served by the motive and consequence of power. Individuals raised in such a power-filled milieu cannot avoid acquiring character tendencies which center on power to some degree. To deny productive expression to these impulses is to force the individual to forego opportunities for self-expresison or compel him to express his strong character tendencies fugitively by acts that incur anxiety and guilt.

The reality of life in a fully managed society suggests that strivings for power and order must cease to be viewed with contempt. As long as their objective necessity is beyond genuine understanding, the malicious and abusive use of power and order will not be properly diagnosed and proper measures will not be taken to control it.

It is folly to deride the autocratic style without due consideration for the motives and consequences that may accompany it. There are many today who view autocracy as a neurotic symptom. Human relations enthusiasts are prone to call the democrat mature, the autocrat immature. However, there are mature autocrats and immature democrats.

The executive holding to the autocratic style may be capable of placing power in the service of order and humanity. He may be firm, efficient, and administratively sensitive, and may suffer from no fewer difficulties in his interpersonal relationships than bureaucrats and democrats. The neurotic, however, is another condition. Whereas it is normal to feel some degree of anxiety, the neurotic executive has these feelings heightened abnormally by the ambiguities which he experiences in the executive role. He must continually struggle to keep proper his interpersonal relationships. Because he is always beset with difficulty, he strives to find a comprehensive solution to which he rigidly adheres but by which his problems are only increased. The ensuing tailspin usually brings on drastic reduction in his effectiveness. Failure is often unavoidable.

Forms of Escape

The individual who feels overwhelmed by the executive role may use many devices to escape from his feelings of anxiety. We have discussed the method of rationalization which is quite common. In addition, the neurotic executive may attempt to escape by denying the existence of anxiety. The pressures and problems of the executive role are discounted in such a way that they do not exist objectively. However, feelings of uncertainty and doubt continue to pervade the unconscious.

The executive who denies his anxieties may seem indifferent to the things that upset most other executives. He may deny the reality of power, the mesmerization of bureaucracy, the moral and human problems of administration. He may deny the restrictiveness of union or government. Whatever pressures exist may be discounted by an optimism that sees the world as much better than it really is. In his refusal to face reality he may succumb to these forces by not effectively meeting their intrinsic and legitimate demands.

This form of escape from anxiety was prevalent among businessmen at the start of the Great Depression. All were sure that "prosperity is just around the corner," "Things could be worse," "All will be better in time." Meanwhile, they conducted business as usual, if they were lucky enough to have a business to conduct during that time of economic depression.

Escape by denial may be manifested in aggressiveness, which is released by actions similar to those of the autocrat. He may throw himself into the face of his supposed villain because he desperately strives to deny that he is the big, mean thing everyone else is afraid of. This reaction is recklessness rather than aggression, and although hostility is usually present, the neurotic greatly overplays the aggression he really feels.

Some business executives vigorously deny that it is difficult to survive in the present system of political and economic restraints. They deny that government is too powerful, that unions are corrupting competition, or that big business is immoral. They ignore these problems or do battle with them with reckless abandon. The president of a business firm recently led his company into an all-out struggle against union demands. Overcoming his anxiety, his long-standing feeling of timidity and helplessness, seemed to be his motivation. By discounting the real power of the union, he was able to summon the necessary courage to fight it. Incidentally, he won.

Another way the executive may escape from intolerable anxiety is to drown it in activity. This executive may control his feelings of uncertainty and insecurity by binding himself to proper and efficient forms of response. Each day he puts himself into the straitjacket of proper response to perform his assignments within the formal requirements and expectation of others. This neurotic is incapable of meeting unexpected events with new and appropriate responses. He relies upon traditional practices, the expertese of his advisors, and the habits and customs of those who face similar problems. In short, he compulsively seeks orderly, rigorous activity aimed at allaying his feelings of anxiety. He adopts a kind of bureaucratic style based on the putting-in complex (see pp. 91–97 and 173–175).

Still another way the executive may escape from administrative anxiety is to withdraw from situations that produce anxiety. This is a radical solution. He may procrastinate on matters that threaten him, delegate these activities to others, or become overly dependent upon his superiors for support and guidance. By this technique the executive finds ways to protect himself. If government restrictions threaten the conduct of his administrative responsibility in a particular area, he arbitrarily chooses to avoid this activity completely, rather than seek out a legitimate opportunity to operate. The same rationale may operate with regard to unions, the public, the consumer, and so forth.

To rationalize, deny, drown in activity, or withdraw from the feelings of administrative anxiety helps the executive avoid admitting that the role he so desperately strives to perform is at base threatening him. In an effort to combat an abnormal amount of administrative anxiety he may use any of the three executive styles. To find release from inner feelings of insecurity and helplessness he may desperately rely upon his own resources or those of specific individuals, including a superior or subordinate; he may be thrown upon the group, which may be an authority-granting body such as a board of directors or a commitee of subordinates; or he may seek refuge in the system of rules and regulations. In short, he may adopt any one or a combination of autocratic, bureaucratic, or democratic styles.

In many cases, the neurotic will acquire an intellectual basis for articulating his administrative style. In such cases, an ideology emerges to give rational support to what is at base an irrational approach to administration. The neurotic acquires a view of the executive role that attempts to accommodate and obviate his inner forces and needs. He is pushed from within rather than directed from without. For him there is but one taskmaster. He must bow down before the inner promptings of a distorted self and all objects and things, including the organization, assume secondary importance before these promptings.

Whatever the forms of escape and whatever the view or style of administrative behavior, they are part of the neurotic's unending search for a comprehensive solution. They are adhered to with increasing rigidity to the detriment of realistic appraisal of and response to events and problems he must face. The resources of the ego, system, or group may become overly taxed to the exclusion of other possible variations and combinations.

Rigidity tends to drive the executive deeper into anxiety, leading to still further commitment to his particular style. He becomes an autocrat, bureaucrat, or democrat not out of choice but out of necessity. It is not that he wants to practice administration in whatever way he adopts, but rather that he must. The neurotic shows an uncommon consistency and persistence in his adherence to his administrative view. He must preserve his format even if it means bending problems and events to accommodate his inflexibility.

The Neurocrat

It would please many people to be able to say authoritatively that because of his unhealthy motives, the neurotic individual cannot succeed in the executive role. This is often the case, but frequently the neurotic does succeed. In fact, neurotic strivings may actually help him to become an effective administrator.

We will use the term neurocrat for those men whose neurotic strivings make them effective administrators. Neurocracy ("neuro" a short form for neurotic and "cracy" meaning type of government or authority) is used to mean an administrative style largely ordered by the neurotic needs and forces within the executive. The neurocrat is a special kind of neurotic, who may practice any of the methods discussed above for concealing his feelings of weakness and insecurity. However, he comes to the executive task because he is neurotic and succeeds mainly for the same reason. Consequently, he may experience anxiety while performing in the executive role, but he performs well in that role because he is already ridden with anxiety.

Neurotic personalities who are incapable of having satisfactory relationships with other people are apt to transfer their frustrations and anxiety into administrative form. They make unilateral claims to power or order or love instead of engaging in spontaneous human interaction. They need a structure that will provide them with the means to deal effectively with their neurotic strivings. However, they are generally unaware of this aspect of their behavior. They are unaware that their need for power, order, or love is so strong that they will do anything to acquire it, including performing effectively within the executive role. Although they may claim the reverse, their value to the organization is only secondary to the executive position itself. It becomes the measure of the man, the end by which all their efforts are justified.

When their neurotic strivings are productively used in performance of the executive role, they set a fast pace for the normal individual whose happiness is less dependent upon the next raise or promotion. The neurocrat's advantage may be too great for many executives of healthy motives who are less ready to pay the price of success. The neurocrat will pay any price.

Of course, many neurotics are not able to perform effectively in the executive role. Neurocrats always seem to balance precariously on the thin edge that separates effective performance from ineffective, and the ordinary neurotic cannot keep himself under sufficient control to walk this tightrope. Then, too, he simply may not want to become a "big" executive and go to the top. The neurocrat, by definition, is capable of translating his neurotic strivings into effective executive performance and does.

Not all who move into business and government and other organizational units are neurocrats. Many are basically well-adjusted persons. Unfortunately, there has been little empirical study of the extent to which neuroticism is a necessity or an aid to success in modern massive organization. Sociologist Professor W. A. Lunden reported in 1960 before the American Association for the Advancement of Science that rulers and bosses are generally smarter and more mentally deranged than other people. He believes that society tends to promote to high positions three types of men: the inadequate antisocial personality, placid and emotionally blunt, often taken for a profound man; the aggressive obsessive-compulsive boss, conceited, ambitious, domineering, and intolerant; the ethically insensitive personality, endowed with acute intelligence but morally wily and cynical.

Dr. Nathan S. Kline, one of several psychiatrists involved in retrospective diagnoses of historical characters, reported that Nero was a full-blown delinquent turned into an adult criminal. Catherine the Great was a compulsive personality, had chronic tension, and escaped by periodic psychosomatic illnesses. Rasputin, the evil genius in the service of the last Russian Czar, was one of the world's most successful psychopaths, whose uncontrolled lust was finally checked by adhering to a doctrine that repentance first required abasement. It has long been said that Cromwell, Robespierre, Hitler, Ford, and

Carnegie all suffered from various degrees of paranoia. Freud is believed to have suffered from hypochondria, Lincoln from melancholia, Napoleon from acute inferiority, and Roosevelt from megalomania.

Lyle M. Spencer, president of Science Research Associates in Chicago, made a study of company presidents under forty who belonged to a club called the Young Presidents Club. His survey showed that they worry most about using power effectively and not being able to do things. They tend to be as dissatisfied with their own work as with that of their most bumbling employees. Many executives maintain a façade that hides this hostility toward themselves and others.

And so the suspicions accumulate that the executive may be more than a quick-witted, hard-driving personality who has earned the respect of the men in his organization. But how neurotic he is or how many are neurotic cannot be determined. The studies we have mentioned are inconclusive because they do not show that neurotic qualities of the executive and rulers are actually the bases of their authority. This condition must be present in neurocracy.

The neurocrat cannot adequately accept the uncertainty and indeterminacy of the executive life. He needs to be certain and secure and responds to the opportunity offered by the executive role as a way to resolve not only a particular conflict, but all conflicts that may arise at a given time.

The neurocrat may picture the executive as the commander of a microcosm. This role promises him not only relief from his painful feelings of inferiority and helplessness, but also realization or fulfillment of himself. He glorifies the executive role beyond realistic proportions. He may show a blind glorification of his superior authorities, or he may deny their right to those high positions to which he aspires. In either case, the neurocrat identifies himself totally with the executive role, and its glorification is merely a projection of his own grandiose self-image. In short, his search for the power, order, or love as an executive is a search for self-glorification.

The neurocrat's drive for glory is typically in utter disregard for his own best interests. The neurotic strives to become a big executive not because of spontaneous wishes or desires. His behavior is not an expression of the real self, but rather is determined by the inner necessities of his neurotic structure. The executive must become a bigger and better executive regardless of his real wishes and better interests. He will sacrifice many things dear to his real self, such as time with his family, his wife, recreation, and relaxation, hobbies, and personal pride and respect.

In other words, the difference between the healthy executive and the neurocrat is one between "I want" and "I must" become a bigger and better executive. The neurocrat has no choice but to drive ahead, seeking, working, fighting, destroying in whatever way will bring him access to the top positions of his organization.

The power, order, or love drive has him in its clutches. He may feel that his working for a promotion is really a genuine choice but actually he is driven to attain it, pushed from within, so to speak. The feelings of complete defeat and humiliation when others rather than he move up offers a clue to his compulsivity to strive for success. And his wanting still more of whatever he is striving for, long after he has surpassed his fondest dreams, offers still another clue to his compulsion to cling to the executive role as his comprehensive solution to life's difficulties.

Power, Order, and Love in the Neurocracy

The neurotic tends to mold his behavior to his idealized picture of the executive role. If he charges the executive role with qualities of power, he will become the complete autocrat. He will dominate and submit at the proper times and in the proper ways with the proper people. He will rule subordinates with an iron hand, show deference and responsiveness to superiors, and uphold the virtues of the organization. The neurocrat does this not because he basically respects power and authority, but because he does not respect it. He does not really see the true utility and social justification of power. All he knows is that power is what he must have, and he will twist himself into any shape to get it.

This neurocrat usually is not able to enter into a give-and-take relationship. He is afraid of initiative in others because he feels he is being left behind if he is not always leading and directing. If his emotions are repressed, it is not because he wishes to control them or the hurt he might inflict on others, but because he wants to succeed and the show of any emotional imbalance might be detrimental to success. He may deprive and exploit at will, but always within the rationality of administrative necessity. He will humiliate and show vindictiveness. Once one gets on his "black list" he never gets off. If the executive can punish for reasons attributable to performance, he will not spare his energy.

Above all, he believes in his feeling of mastery. He holds the conviction that there is nothing he cannot do and no one he cannot win. He is often charming to the point of being understanding and graceful. He can be splendidly wicked. The need for total triumph reveals his lack of genuine feelings of intimacy and affection. It so happens that when his neurotic striving for power is productively contained, he may appear to be a courageous, fearless, decisive, reliable man upon whom others rely for support and guidance. He may be just the man that others feel is needed as their chief executive.

The neurotic bureaucrat clings to his bounded area of expertese, rules, and procedures for his effectiveness and security. He will practice administration and perhaps personal tidiness, routine regularity, accuracy, and reliability with vigor and zeal. But he does not seem to get a kick out of his being systematic. He derives no satisfaction from being able to help someone in need or engage in a mutual administrative purpose. He is not capable of relaxing and being satisfied with himself, because he is dominated by an unconscious policeman who threatens to punish him if he fails to be proper and correct in all his affairs. The only reward seems to be a momentary relief from the belaboring pangs of insignificance and impropriety. In these moments of relief he may feel like a "big-shot" executive who is in command of vast systems of human endeavor. While sitting in his immaculately arranged office, he is unaware that behind these intermittent feelings of glory and power lies the desire to become all powerful.

This neurocrat moves rigidly and consistently toward perfection. What really matters is not the petty details, but the flawless excellence of the whole conduct of his administrative responsibility. Because he is just and dutiful, he is entitled to just and dutiful treatment from others. The conviction that an infallible justice operates within the administrative system of which he is a part allows him to give his total loyalty to it and to encourage others, boss, peers, and subordinates, to serve it zealously.

In an age when the system plays a crucial role in giving productive and efficient expression to resources of the company, government, or association, this neurocrat may be well received. He may be the organization man whose infectious mannerisms allow the spread of his disease to engulf others who unconsciously desire to put themselves into the safe arms of an omniscient and omnipotent system. Outwardly he is the master who uses the system for the welfare of those concerned; inwardly, he needs the system to contain and regiment his untrustworthy, immoral impulses for power.

But an organization is more than power and order. It provides a network of human interrelationships that tend toward permanence and mutuality. The neurotic drive for affection and affiliation may also cause the individual to locate in structures and depend upon them as much as the power-packed personality.

This neurocrat represents not the appeal of power, but the appeal of love. He wants desperately to be well received, liked, approved. He glorifies the executive as one who is loved, sets out to become that very person, and makes use of his role for this purpose. Although he craves affection, naturally he does not consciously say to himself or others, "I need to be loved." Superficial masculinity found in the glorification of his role as a big executive does not allow entertaining such obviously effeminate thoughts. He is forced to put his demands for affection on some administrative basis.

He may develop an administrative format subtly aimed at acquiring the loyalty, respect, and devotion of others. His aim is to be loved both as a person and as an executive. He must not consciously feel superior to others or display any such feelings in his behavior. He will shun any thought, feeling, or gesture of acquiring power for itself.

His administrative format will attempt to present all the qualities of democracy. He will share all he has with others, emphasize freedom, practice equality, and entertain rational modes of decision-making, including group deliberation. His crucial acts of compromise will, for all practical purposes, be oriented toward the realistic and objective needs of the organization. Rather than resenting the initiative of others, he thoroughly expects it. He is to be the object of their respect, devotion, and loyalty. Even when making perfectly legitimate requests he may feel that he is taking advantage of others.

He practices self-minimizing to the point that he leans over backward to avoid anything which seems arrogant, conceited, or presumptuous. It is conceit to think that he can make decisions alone, that he is the one to whom all must be responsible. He consistently seeks out others to help in this or that detail. He may neglect his own ends, needs, and appearances, and conversely, he may display considerable energy and skill in attaining things for others. He is in many respects a good committee chairman, team man, company man.

But like the neurocrat who is driven by power, he does not achieve give-and-take relationships. He preaches and practices democracy, but he is not really free himself. He is so totally dependent upon the affection of others that he is enslaved by them. He cannot do without them and attempts to make sure that they cannot do without him. Inwardly he needs the executive role as a crutch to give his life meaning and purpose.

In short, the power, order, and love impulses in their neurotic forms may help the executive surmount and master the pressures that play havoc with the executive role. The methods of defending himself against anxiety, including rationalization and denial, may allow the neurocrat to remain relatively unaware that the role which he so aggressively performs is at base threatening to him. While outwardly displaying a love for the executive role, he is inwardly made to feel insecure by it. His anxiety assures that he will work all the harder to be a successful executive. Hence, the neurocrat is apt to succeed where the ordinary neurotic may be overwhelmed and discouraged.

The ordinary neurotic's feelings of helplessness may become hopelessness because there is not enough success in his executive role. The neurocrat is able to express his neurotic strivings productively. Consequently, his anxiety does not reach the advanced stage of depression. Neurocrats seem uncommonly zestful and alert where ordinary neurotics may be lethargic and slow. In many cases the neurocrat appears to be healthy and mature and very much the ideal executive that others identify with as their ego-ideal. The neurocrat has learned to put his emotional disturbances to work for him in his administrative role. He succeeds because he is neurotic.

The Flexible Executive

We have seen that the neurotic may be dominated by the need to be an effective executive at all costs. His style represents a comprehensive solution to the ambiguities of the executive role. The acquisition of power or expertese or acceptance or any combination of these qualities means that he will no longer feel uncertainty, insignificance, and humiliation. Whenever he chooses to zig, he will not be countered by pressures to zag; whenever he chooses to dominate, he will not be rebuked for being dictatorial; whenever he chooses to control, he will not be thwarted by demands for service. He wants assurance that whatever he does will not require adjustments and changes. He wants to be free of the need to be flexible.

The neurotic has no internal check on whatever gains he may make in overcoming the ambiguity of the executive role. He does not check his drive for power, order, or love. The problem that the neurotic presents to his organization or society is that he must be kept upright; he cannot stand upright by his own resources. There have been enough of these men in the past to justify the present network of entangling restrictions that have been placed on the business executive. What our society needs is not more neurocrats, but rather healthy, responsible executives who will strive to become useful and who know the true boundaries of their administrative and social responsibilities so that these responsibilities do not have to be pointed out to them by more rules and regulations, taboos and restraints.

Specifically, the executive type needed to cope with the growing problems and pressures of an organized society is oriented toward reality. He obeys the reality principle, that is, the objective needs and demands of his people, organization, and society are in unquestionable control. He is their servant, not because he feels weak, immoral, alone, or insignificant, but because he feels strong, united with them, and responsible for them. He controls them not because he has failed to master the authorities of his past, but because he has learned to serve the authorities of the present.

Consequently, he is not overly anxious about the ambiguity of having to limit his control to the function of providing a socially responsible service or product, or limiting his service to the administrative responsibility of controlling the people and resources at his command to maintain and perpetuate their better interests. He is not afraid of flexibility.

To serve by controlling and control by serving requires inner restraints. The flexible man has control over himself, that is, control over the forces that constitute and attempt to influence the self. He exerts self-control by achieving an administrative balance, preserving and strengthening that balance against disruptive tendencies, and carefully expanding it to accommodate new skills.

This does not mean that the flexible executive changes with each minute variation in the unfolding administrative situation. This would constitute such a high degree of erraticism and unpredictability that the executive would cease to be a source of stable influence and control. To be sure, the fluctuations are severe and numerous enough at times for the executive to almost lose self-control.

However, he may achieve and maintain self-control by using an amalgam of the three executive styles. Once he arrives at this amalgam through years of trial and error, he will not have to vary it except when his testing of reality shows ample justification. The amalgam by its very nature implies flexibility because it has been strategically drawn from what the executive feels to be the most productive ingredients of all three executive styles.

To repeat, what differentiates the neurotic from the flexible man is the degree to which the executive is directed by irrational forces within or by realistic and objective needs and demands from without. Of course, in many cases we cannot determine to what degree the individual is responsive to internal or external forces. We are dealing with qualities that defy exact measurement. Nevertheless, we can easily identify the two extremes. On the one hand, we see the neurotic rigidity of Hitler, who could not perceive reality as it existed but attempted to rationalize it, deny it, or make it over. On the other hand, we have the example of Churchill, who had great insight into the objective circumstances and their demands. Consequently, Churchill could anticipate Hitler's moves with greater accuracy than Hitler could anticipate Churchill's. These two historical figures differed in their ability to comprehend events and conditions and to control their human impulses to achieve mastery of reality. No doubt this difference played a decisive role in the outcome of the war.

We can cite many examples of the flexible executive in business and governmental administration. George M. Humphrey, former Secretary of the Treasury and a powerful figure in Eisenhower's administration, is a realist who thinks a problem must be dealt with in the light of the way things are rather than as he would like them to be. For example, Humphrey is a conservative. Nevertheless, as board chairman of the M. A. Hanna Company he and Benjamin Fairless averted a coal strike in 1947 by signing an agreement so favorable to the mine workers that it was regarded by many coal operators as a betrayal. Unruffled, Humphrey pointed out that he was dealing with a reality. If he had refused a settlement, there would have been a long costly work stoppage, at the end of which the miners still would have gotten from the government what they originally wanted.[4]

Keeping in touch with reality is exactly what the neurotic cannot do. Stalin seized the party apparatus and made it the vehicle of his own neurotic ambitions for total power. Having mastered the party he completely transformed a group of idealists into a group of sycophants or yes-men who gradually lost their hold on reality. Then he attempted to bludgeon and bully the world with inadequate appreciation of the material he was hammering away at.

In contrast, Khrushchev is an empiricist who uses all the means that come to hand in the shrewd service of realistic opportunities and demands. He has placed his government in contact with the western world by transforming a party of yes-men back into a party of practical leaders. He relies heavily

[4] "George Humphrey? Of Course," *Fortune*, January, 1953, p. 176.

on his administrative subordinates to the point of appearing at times to seek them out for advice. During his lengthy press conference in Paris when he announced that the summit talks would not proceed because of the U-2 incident, he seemed to be taking his cues directly from the military attaché seated next to him. Contrary to interpretation that he was no longer in the driver's seat, Khrushchev was so much in control that he felt secure enough to accept consultation. Insecure men are seldom flexible. Whereas Stalin would never leave Russia for fear that while he was gone he would be overthrown, Khrushchev seems quite secure while traveling abroad.

Both Stalin and Khrushchev were made of steel, but Stalin was molded in the form of a hammer and Khrushchev in the form of a spring. Unfortunately, Khrushchev is so flexible that he has managed to set the west back on its heels. Stalin's myopic Czech purge and Berlin blockade frightened the west into achieving military unity and economic cooperation. Rather than menace, Khrushchev uses more subtle methods, including offering loans and technical assistance, shaving interest rates, and playing the role of a genial Russian Father Frost to the underdeveloped nations.[5] His insight into the world psyche was displayed in asking the uncommitted nations to be neutral in the contest between the east and the west. Although Dulles had declared that neutrality was immoral and shortsighted, Khrushchev was so effective in winning nations to his views that Eisenhower was forced publicly to disagree with his secretary of state. Kennedy has adopted Khrushchev's game of enticing nations by recognizing their legitimate rights to neutrality.

[5] Joseph G. Harrison, "Khrushchev Formidable Opponent," *The State Journal*, January 21, 1961.

Events seem to be going Khrushchev's way, mostly because he has been able to see and meet the realistic opportunities to which Stalin was blind. He is in this year 1961 calling the tune to which the west must dance. Unfortunately, his superior realism may be the deciding factor in who calls and who dances in the next decade. Flexibility grounded in the reality principle can be a powerful tool in the hands of the executive.

Executive Maturity Today

In summary, the attempt to blend the three potentially antagonistic executive styles into a smooth, rhythmic whole is not easy. Ambiguity results which is far greater than any anticipated by the autocrats of the past. It is a mark of maturity to be able to tolerate such ambiguity. Although many executives are overwhelmed by feelings of uncertainty and doubt, many are attempting to relate productively to the changing shape of events and conditions. They may be anxious, as are most people today, but it is questionable whether they are neurotic. However, the danger is that more neurotics will be attracted to the executive role or more executives will become neurotic because of the ambiguity in their role. This danger may increase because of the lack of adequate study of the emotional problems of executives.

What best identifies the neurotic executive today is his attempt to find a comprehensive solution that does away with all ambiguity and uncertainty. He may blow his horn for autocracy, bureaucracy, or democracy. In his total support of the power theme, for example, he reveals an inability to accept the fact that he is involved in a network of human relationships that require cooperation and team work. Or in his total support of the democratic theme, he is unable to accept the social and moral necessity of power and order. Or in his total castigation of the bureaucratic trend, he is unable to accept the basic necessity for order and efficiency.

If his style is supplemented with ingredients from the other two, he is not conscious of the degree to which his administrative format exceeds his view of the proper executive role. There are executives who talk about democracy in business and their support of good human relations practices. Yet within their administrative context they are autocrats. Many publicly decry bureaucracy and the civil service mentality, but yet show an incapacity in their administrative activities to rely upon their own resources. Besides misleading people and giving faulty advice, these neurotics encourage others to seek a safe, sure formula of half-baked gimmicks.

In our present era of rapid change and grave uncertainty, there are many who are quick to grasp at supposedly sure-fire ideas and techniques. Whether these newly acquired possessions succeed or fail, the individual continues to seek more well-proved administrative gadgets. So acutely are they stricken with administrative anxiety that they hurry from one gimmick to the next, never certain of whatever progress they are making.

If one were to believe the public statements and writings of leading administrators, one could believe that most of them are genuinely anchored in the democratic style. Few will openly admit being autocratic or bureaucratic. After all, this is the age of the enlightened executive who assumes his social responsibility. However, upon close inspection they show a tendency to cling to the democratic theme out of feelings of inadequacy and uncertainty. They are democrats out of fear of public opinion rather than because they genuinely understand the needs and problems of people.

The neurotic does not recognize that if he is successful at all, his success is due to the very things that he tends to reject or is unaware of. Stalin rejected the idea that subordinates have thoughts of their own. Yet, subordinates rescued him from many of his own blunders by daring to have their own thoughts. If Stalin had been able to accept the need for competence among his subordinates, he would have been less autocratic. However, the needs of his neurotic structure required that he acknowledge himself as the source of all competence.

In the administrative sense the flexibility to adapt to the realistic situation confronting the executive allows him greater opportunity to perform his role responsibly and reliably. We have illustrated this point in Chapter 3. Truman, for example, showed an amazing capacity to withhold his arbitrary tendencies by entering into a distinctly team effort on the development of the Marshall Plan. However, he showed an incapacity to be arbitrary with MacArthur when the latter initiated aggressive action aimed at usurping the president's authority as Commander in Chief. Stephen P. Kennedy, formerly of the New York City Police Department, was arbitrary on all issues. His demise is representative of what happens when one becomes totally immersed in a set style.

With things as they are today, dogmatic support of a narrowly based administrative style is actually a flight from reality or a distortion of reality to conform to one's inner forces and needs. However, the executive may feel that he is in contact with reality when he upholds one view to the exclusion of all others. He cannot be argued out of his position because his argument is not based upon the situation as it is, but as it appears to him. And because he is not capable of entering into shared experiences, he is not able to rid himself of his distorted picture. He will go about preaching his cause, completely unaware that he is arbitrarily dictating for everyone the conditions of their performance without regard to their unique qualities. He supports his pet view with intractable vigor. While he exalts freedom, he keeps a closed mind.

Although the changing, dynamic administrative scene of today requires flexibility, this does not mean being wishy-washy. The flexible man is firm when the nature of the situation requires firmness or the purposes for which he stands require vigorous action. Nor does flexibility mean being without order. The flexible man knows when bureaucratic techniques are required and knows how to use them in the service of his administrative responsibility. Nor does flexibility mean unconditional permissiveness. The flexible executive practices freedom and equality, shares himself on the basis of the mutual interests of the individual and the organization. He is firm, however, when the continued unity and productive cohesiveness of the group are threatened by the power ambitions or compulsive orderliness of others. In short, the ideal executive today blends autocracy, bureaucracy, and democracy into an effective administrative style that can be adapted to meet the evolving needs and problems of his administrative responsibility.

Few executives have the capacity to be as mobile as this picture of the flexible executive. The typical executive will, in all likelihood, be more firmly anchored in one of the three styles. We have noted in the previous chapter that, in spite of their public statements, many executives are basically bureaucrats who supplement their style with ingredients of autocracy and democracy. As bad as this amalgam may seem to those who favor the democratic style, it is not nearly as bad as the executive who is totally committed to the bureaucratic style. The great danger to our society is not that executives are acquiring bureaucratic tendencies, but that they might not acquire at the same time sufficient ingredients of the other two styles. The rigidity and narrowmindedness that might result from total immersion in the bureaucratic style would be lethal at this time when our society must chart new goals and find new and better human combinations with which to survive and win the struggle with world communism. Similarly, total immersion in the democratic style would present disadvantages just as fatal. Too much reliance upon the group can weaken still further the executive's already weakened sense of personal responsibility for his organization's deeds and acts.

From an administrative point of view, democracy is as potentially dangerous as autocracy and bureaucracy. There is no guarantee that democracy will not create problems just as severe as those created by the autocrats of the past and by bureaucratic tendencies in executives today. The intense activity of executives to broaden their administrative base to include substantial ingredients of democracy reflects the capacity to be more flexible than their predecessors. However, the problems that may develop may be quite severe. Only time will tell whether the flexible administrative style is a decided improvement. However, it does seem to offer more to the executive than any one executive style.

In conclusion, the flexible man is the legitimate heir to the rigid administrative style of the past. The autocrat was best suited to a simple, unambiguous society and organization. When society and organization became larger and more complex, the autocrat failed to respond to the changing scene. He rationalized and denied his growing feelings of uncertainty and doubt rather than confront them to discover why they existed and what should be done about them.

The fall of the businessman in the depression, the rise of big unions, the emergence of an enlightened public, and the heavy hand of government have contributed to making the business executive role an intensely ambiguous responsibility. How, when, and whom to serve and control are not easily decided. A well-proportioned administrative mix, seasoned carefully by ingredients from all three styles is needed. But the proper amalgam depends upon the individual and his particular administrative situation. The mature executive is prepared to accept this flexibility in light of his realistic understanding of the new and changing problems that confront the executive role.

The neurotic will reject this conclusion as insufficient because it spells out nothing specific upon which he can reliably base his administrative style. His desire for a comprehensive solution will not tolerate the recognition that what may work for one may not for another. The strain in the executive role forces him to depend on himself, his system, or his group, or a set combination of the three to the exclusion of amendments that productively express his genuine self and relate to his peculiar administrative situation. He acquires an administrative style not out of reason and choice, but out of inner necessity.

INDEX